Wilderness Awakenings
A Photo Journal of Spiritual Awakening

Joseph F. Classen

Copyright © 2019 Joseph F. Classen

All rights reserved. No part of this written or photographic publication may be reproduced, stored in a retrieval system or transmitted in any form or by any means without the prior written permission of the publisher.

ISBN-13: 978-1-7082-0372-6

Wild Revelation Outdoors
www.wildrevelation.com

DEDICATION

Tom F. Classen
July 21, 1933 – Oct 27, 2018

    This book is dedicated in loving memory of my dad, Tom F. Classen. Out of all the books I have written over the years, the first edition of this book (which came out in 2014) was among my dad's favorite. He never said exactly why he enjoyed it so much, but I suspect it was because it reminded him of the many things he treasured about spending time in the solitude and beauty of nature…things which he reflected on often throughout his life, and things he sought to instill in me as I grew up.

    Dad had a great sense of adventure and an undying appreciation for the things that could be discovered in the tranquil silence of the woods and the water. Whether it was a relaxing hike through the colorful autumn forests, kayaking one of the many rivers or lakes of Missouri, or fly fishing for whatever fish would accept his finely feathered offering, all those activities were simply catalysts for experiencing something much more profound. What, exactly, those profound things were, I didn't fully understand as a youngster. However, as I grew into adolescence and adulthood, I would eventually unravel those mysteries for myself, which I now continually strive to share with others through books like this one. Thanks, Dad, for having the patience to help me learn and appreciate the ways of the wilderness.

CONTENTS

Dedication	Page 1
Introduction	Page 6
Chapter One - *Earthly Paradise*	Page 8

Entering into an Alaskan paradise
The beauty of nature evoking a spiritual response

Chapter Two - *Oh my God!* — Page 14

Nature as the greatest work of art
Instinctively recognizing the Creator in creation
The gifts that nature offers humanity
The Divine artist
The elusive artist
Self-reliance VS God-reliance
Caring for creation

Chapter Three - *Hell on Earth* — Page 26

Experiencing the worst in nature: a reality check
The incarnate wisdom of the wilderness
The wild relationship

Chapter Four - *Trailhead* — Page 32

The wilderness as a place of divine encounter and education
The wilderness as a place of hidden evil
The indifference of nature
Indifference promoting positive choices

Chapter Five - *Let There Be Light* — Page 36

Sunrise
Living in the light
A light in the darkness

Chapter Six - *The Adventure of Adventure* — Page 42

The thrill of preparing for a wilderness adventure
Precautionary measures
The natural high
Back down to earth

Chapter Seven - *Become Water*   Page 50
The transforming power of water
Wisdom from water

Chapter Eight - *Listening*   Page 54
Listening to the wilderness
Hearing VS listening
The vital importance of stillness and silence

Chapter Nine - *Cycle of Life*   Page 58
The reality of life and death in nature
The regenerative powers of nature
Get busy living

Chapter Ten - *Open Your Eyes*   Page 64
The difference between vision and merely seeing
Appreciating overlooked, unrecognized beauty

Chapter Eleven - *Wild Freedom*   Page 68
The life of an eagle
Natural freedom

Chapter Twelve - *Right Now*   Page 72
Encountering wildlife
Living and appreciating a life lived in the now

Chapter Thirteen - *From the Wilderness to the World*   Page 76
Human wilderness dwellers
The roots of a wilderness monk
Q & A with a hermit
The eremitic life
The spirituality of a hermit
Back to the world

ABOUT THE AUTHOR

Joseph Classen has connected with audiences throughout the world by means of his numerous books and magazine articles on topics including outdoor skills, nature & wildlife photography, and Christian spirituality. He was the host of a nationally syndicated outdoors-themed radio show for several years, is currently involved in a variety of freelance media projects and is a member of the *Professional Outdoor Media Association*. Joseph has worked with some of the top conservation biologists in the world and his photography and writing have been featured by prestigious organizations such as *National Geographic* and *Smithsonian*.

Along with his media work, he is also an experienced Alaskan wilderness guide and consultant, specializing in nature & wildlife photography, fishing, hunting, and outdoor adventure. To see and learn more, please visit *Wild Revelation Outdoors* at www.wildrevelation.com

"Everybody needs beauty as well as places to play in and pray in, where nature may heal and give strength to body and soul."

John Muir

"Our heart is restless until it rests in you."

St. Augustine.

INTRODUCTION

Wilderness Awakenings has been many years in the making. From the dawning of my life, I have been intensely drawn to wild places and what they offer humanity. A great deal of whom and what I am today has been lovingly shaped, and sometimes harshly forged, from spending quality time in the natural world.

The bulk of this book was originally written in June through September of 2013. The better part of those four months was spent living and working deep in the remote Alaskan wilderness of Kodiak Island…a place that would eventually become my home. It was a time of major change, reflection, and transition in my life, both personally and professionally. I desperately needed time and space to clear my head and purify my soul. And, there was no better place to do so than the wilderness.

Those four months ultimately brought tremendous healing and renewal, and also reignited my desire to write a book about the interconnectedness and relationship between God, humanity, and creation. Not only to write about it…but also to share it photographically, as "a picture is worth a thousand words." Many of the photographs included in the chapters of this book were taken in the field, on location while in the process of actually writing the original rough draft. Other photos are those that I took at different times and places all over Alaska and the lower 48, which are simply meant to illustrate the themes of each chapter.

My extended stay in the wild was an unforgettable experience. Modern modes of communication were extremely minimal, and in most cases, were not available at all. I would often encounter more bears than people on any particular day…sometimes for weeks on end. While environmental issues are popular in the mainstream media today, many of those who write about them often present a rather "Disney-ish" perception of wilderness and wildlife. The reality of living *in* and *with* truly wild nature for long periods of time is something quite different. Few ever experience this reality firsthand. The experience is both beautiful and brutal. This reality is also something that I hope to share in this book.

I'd like to thank those few people who I shared those months with. I am forever grateful for your companionship and hospitality. I would also especially like to thank Rev. Robert Matter, a Trappist monk and priest (now deceased) who lived alone in the wilderness of the Ozark Mountains for many years and was gracious enough to grant me an interview with him back in 2008…which finally made it to print.

This book was originally released exclusively as an eBook in 2014 under a similar title, *Awakenings in the Wild*. It never made it to print though, as the publishers that I was working with at the time felt that a rather large-scale publication of a full-color print book would be far too expensive of a project. Much has changed since then, thankfully. The book has been revised and updated, and I now operate my own media business, which has opened the door for this book to finally be available in print form, as well as an updated eBook version for all of you digital readers. I hope you enjoy this collection of essays and photographs (all of which are also available as limited edition fine art prints) and I warmly invite you to see and learn more by visiting *Wild Revelation Outdoors* at www.wildrevelation.com

Sincerely,

Joseph Classen

CHAPTER 1
EARTHLY PARADISE

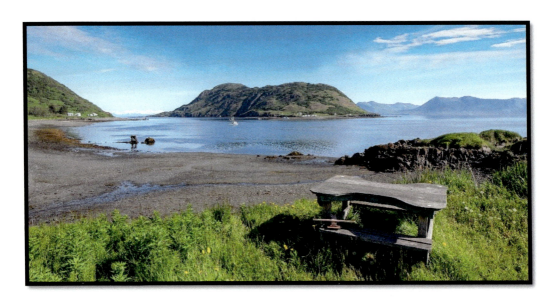

Have I entered paradise? As I write these words, it is a spectacular, cool, spring morning. I'm seated on an old, weather-beaten picnic table overlooking Uyak Bay on Kodiak Island, Alaska. Right beside me, a rather tame red fox just emerged from the tall grass, giving me a curious, but friendly look, and then it moved on in search of breakfast and the rest of her family.

As I glance up from my scribbled handwriting and look across the bay, I see a young bald eagle perched on a rocky ridge staring right back at me. I see great expanses of coastal mountains covered in lush green grass sitting beneath the towering shadows of their larger snowcapped siblings. Above them is a tapestry of endless blue sky, smoky white clouds that constantly change shape in the winds, and bursts of bright yellow sunshine which breaks through amidst the shifting heavens.

In the not too far off distance, through a window of steep, cascading hillsides, I can see the intimidating waters of the Shelikof Straight. Beyond it is the Katmai Coast, and the jagged peaks of the Alaska Peninsula. Along the tide ravaged beaches, nestled in the more protected areas of the landscape, are fishing and hunting camps, long-abandoned trapper's cabins, the wreckage of an old ship, and a rotting boat dock from days gone by.

Drifting in the rolling blue waters before me are salmon fishing skiffs, gill nets protruding out from the banks, tendering boats, and bright orange buoys marking the location of strategically placed gear. In the depths below them are thousands of salmon on the way to their spawning grounds, halibut and cod roaming the ocean floor, and a myriad of different species of fish. Along the other side of the bay, I see the deceivingly calm water being interrupted by the spouting and breaching of a variety of whales, both monstrously big and surprisingly small. In the shallow coves and sheltered beaches around them are sea otters floating on their oily backs amidst the rocking waters, seemingly without a care in the world. Resting on top of tiny islands that are emerging from the lowering tide are chubby harbor seals. Alone, or with their families, they sun themselves and take a break after the morning hunt for fish.

Washed up and scattered about on the beach are starfish, crabs, clams, and shellfish of all kinds. Mixed in with them are slimy, gelatinous jellyfish, huge bundles of tangled bull and finger kelp, and the remains of other creatures that became food for the more dominant.

Speeding across the surface of the water like fighter planes in attack formation are groups of colorful puffins, and a great variety of waterfowl. High above them are graceful eagles, crafty ravens and crows, acrobatic seagulls and larger birds, all in search of a bite to eat and a place to rest for a while.

Nestled in the tall grass, thick weeds, and the bushy terrain of the land around me, I hear an orchestra of songbirds, each sweetly whistling their own unique tune in rhythm with the tempo of the crashing waves. Yet, when all perform together, it is not atonal bedlam, but rather a perfect, natural harmony. In a similar manner, decorating the hills and the valleys are summer wildflowers of all shapes, sizes, and colors…each one distinctly different from the next, yet when combined together on the canvas of creation, there is not a mess of cluttered, abstract confusion, but rather a masterpiece of organized, artistic allure. Among the blades of grass and colorful blooms, there is yet another intricate world in motion. Busy bees and countless insects are all out and about, hard at work, and making the most of the long Alaskan days.

In the miles upon miles of secretive wilderness behind me are blacktail deer cautiously moving along their well-worn trails, as half-ton Kodiak brown bears…the mighty kings of this land…saunter through the alder thickets, demanding the respect of all. Rabbits, squirrels, and other rodents scamper and hop about, always on the lookout for those in the forest who would love to have them for dinner…and not as a guest. Looking down on it all are bands of snow-white mountain goats, hunkered in along the steep ridges of the surrounding summits.

When I pause to take in a deep breath of fresh island air, I can sense the pleasing bouquet of burning firewood from the camp stove and the fragrance of the wildflowers mixed with the salty sea breeze. I can detect the scent of fish, both fresh and old, the pollen from the summer vegetation and the budding trees. When I walk through the untamed land around me, I can smell the musky odor of nearby bears and the rotting bits of flesh left on the bones from one of their previous meals. With a closer olfactory inspection, I can detect where the deer have recently moved through. I can catch a whiff of their freshly cut tracks in the earth and the sharply nipped ends of newly chewed vegetation.

In such a setting, all five senses are pleasingly stimulated to the maximum. In a word, it is paradise, or at least as close as I have been able to get to it here on earth. However, being in such a stunningly pristine, far-beyond beautiful, natural environment does not simply evoke mere sensory euphoria…it goes much deeper than that. It penetrates into the core of one's being, and into the recesses of one's soul. I have no doubt whatsoever that the *Creator* consciously *created* us to recognize, and participate in the artistry of *creation*. Beholding the magnificence of nature in such a manner beckons forth, and even demands, a true spiritual response.

(Photograph locations: Uyak Bay and the surrounding areas of Kodiak Island, Alaska)

CHAPTER 2
"OH MY GOD!"

My formal education is in the disciplines of philosophy and theology. Those fields of study, coupled with my lifelong obsession with the great outdoors, have devoutly instilled within me the belief that there is no greater art than that which is found in nature. Faith, scientific reason, and vast personal experience have all taught me that there is no greater artist than the Creator, God Almighty, from which all beauty, and the very ability to recognize it, comes forth. Without exception, all of humanity is hard-wired to appreciate the captivating allure of creation.

Natural beauty is something that goes far beyond the intellect. It reaches deep down into the heart and soul. It is divine, transcendent, and powerfully inspirational. We all have a similar reaction when beholding something magnificently beautiful…there is a sudden pause, and an instant halting of our being that commands us to treasure what is before us. Upon witnessing the stunning sight of natural artistry, our jaws drop, and our hearts skip a beat. We quickly inhale a breath of fresh air, and our facial muscles relax. At such moments, our pupils dilate in unbridled attraction as we proclaim, "Oh my God! Look at THAT!" It is interesting to note how we naturally speak the name of God at such times, and not in vain! Whether we admit it or not, whether it is conscious or unconscious, I propose that we all instinctively know the source of such beauty.

Spending time in nature does something very positive, constructive, and healing to us. It is a catalyst for peace and tranquility. As we sit in the predawn darkness and watch the sun come up and the world come alive, something in *us* comes alive. We experience the hope and glory of a new beginning. As the sun sets in the evening and lights the sky on fire, we can't help but to feel the calming satisfaction of a restful end.

It's in the wilderness that the lovely tune of songbirds evokes sweetness in our hearts, while an encounter with a dangerous beast fills us with instant respect. The tenderness of a mother with her young reminds us of the universal power of love. The caressing sound of the ocean waves, the trickling of a mountain stream, and the hypnotic trance of the rain lapses our souls into a state of divine calm. Our troubles and fears are gently washed away and our hearts purified. The fascinating mystery of the stars and the antiquity of the moon summons forth an appreciation of the eternal. Admiring the seemingly simple lives of wildlife brings us comfort and escape, as we wish our hectic lives were only so peaceful.

Creation possesses an incarnation of wisdom and offers an invitation for one to learn its ways…though it must be tamed and tempered by virtue and reason. The wilderness is a place of education where we can be challenged, disciplined, and can expand the mind, body, and soul. It serves as a *universal university* where one learns to embrace, appreciate, and revere the gift and purpose of life…all life, but most especially that of human life, as we are the caretakers of the rest of creation. The lessons learned in nature must not stay in the wild to die alone and be forgotten like the creatures that live there. The transcendent beauty experienced in the gallery of creation must be shared and cherished by others.

The Divine Artist

When we consider the astounding, intricate beauty, the stunning engineering, and the mind-boggling complexity that is present in all of creation, it becomes undeniable that a master artist has been consciously at work, that such jaw-dropping wonder simply can't be a random, cosmic mistake. Even when considering purely scientific explanations for creation, such as the *theory of evolution*, we have to ask if this process in and of itself can be solely responsible for making such incredible magnificence out of gas, dirt, proteins, and enzymes which were just aimlessly floating around out there in space or lying on a beach. If so, those initial materials and those processes would then have to be perfectly designed ones to begin with. While it's obvious that living things evolve and adapt according to their environment, the very ability to do so is utterly amazing!

The processes of creation and forces of nature act quite similar to those of an artist who is painting a masterpiece. It begins with a pallet that is filled with what looks like a complete mess, with globs of paint slopped about and mixed together in ways that are anything but pleasing to the eye. The canvas is at first cluttered with abrasive strokes and only hints of emerging composition, structure, and beauty. However, upon completion, we stand back in awe and again proclaim, "Oh, my God! Look at that!"

On a deeper level, when meditating on the subject of creation and the creative processes that are an ongoing part of it, consider the fact that scientists have discovered that the odds of DNA assembling by mere chance are ten thousand to one. Other scientists proclaim that it isn't so much a matter of "chance," but that it's rather a combination of the laws of physics, nuclear force, electromagnetism and gravity. But, being that laws of any kind are also things that are initially created, who is responsible for making these laws which govern the universe? Who would have known that we needed them? Around and around we go! When it's all said and done, what are we left with? We are left with a mystery that we will never solve. We are left with the obvious realization that it is simply impossible for *everything* to come from *nothing*. That *"everything,"* in all of its incredible glory, is ultimately the essence of God.

The Elusive Artist

For as long as rational humans have walked the earth, they have searched for ways to better understand, recognize, and grasp this divine essence, which is perceived and experienced as God. Throughout the ages, humankind has desperately tried to prove, or disprove, God's existence. There have been countless books written and complex intellectual arguments presented on this topic. Philosophers, theologians, and scientists have debated and wrestled over the existence of God for centuries upon centuries, right up until this very day.

At times, it seems as if the subject of God is an ongoing, societal tug of war game. Some eras bring about a heightened awareness and appreciation for things of a spiritual or theological nature, and others, like our current day, appear to be increasingly swaying to the side of a rather godless, atheistic culture…grossly overlooking the fact that science and religion *are not* opposed to each other, but rather, they work wonderfully together with the proper application and perspective.

Once again, when all is considered, what is the end result of all the intellectual pugilism over the topic of the Almighty? The same as what we began with, which is a great mystery that will not, and cannot, be solved by the arrogant thinking of mere mortals. There will never be "proof" for the existence of God that will satisfy all…one way or the other. At the same time though, with the eyes of faith and common sense, we can learn much about our Creator, as all of creation tells us something about the one who created it.

As a master tracker can objectively know a great deal about a particular animal he is on the trail of without actually seeing it, we can learn a tremendous amount about God from being aware of, and following the "signs" of creation. In a likewise fashion, we can know much about the interior and external personality of a human being from what he or she has made and from the ideas that inspired his or her creation. Works of art, for example, whether they are of music, painting, writing, etc., can tell us what psychological, spiritual, emotional, and even physical state the person who created them was in. We can discover an artist's intentions, feelings, and thoughts by carefully studying their masterpiece. Art and creative work of any kind makes an intentional, sometimes subtle, sometimes bold, personal statement.

This phenomenon takes place on a much simpler level, as well. Walk into someone's home and you can tell much about the owner from how their surroundings are organized or decorated. Notice how a particular person prepares their food, cleans up after themselves, or what their work ethic is like and you will discover much about that person. No matter who that individual is, even if he or she is shrouded in a cloud of mystery and we just can't figure them out or learn what makes them tick, if enough time is spent, if enough careful, detailed observation is implemented, one will eventually discover who and what a person is all about. The same applies to God. We see the basics of who and what God is like from observing and studying the Almighty's engineering, creation, organization, efficiency, sense of beauty, and even the Creator's sense of humor. Why is it that the ugliest, creepiest things on earth like a king crab, halibut, black cod, or a big dirty catfish are the tastiest?

Self-Reliance VS God-Reliance

The phenomena of experiencing the Creator through creation is one that indigenous/aboriginal people knew well, as they were a society with a great connection to the earth and all of creation. Thus, they recognized the obvious role and importance that the Creator played. While many of these cultures of peoples were an extremely self-reliant lot, they realized that the "self" could only do so much. More so, they became a "God-reliant" people, as all the raw materials that they needed to live and survive ultimately came from creation, as it still does today. Like the native peoples of our world, when one spends countless hours in creation, relying on creation, observing creation, working with creation, respecting creation, and properly using creation, one comes to know in a very real way the Creator and enters into a true relationship with God.

On the other side of the coin, when one lives a life far removed from nature, strictly in a "manmade" world, a great disconnectedness with both creation and the Creator comes about. When we live complex lives in a rather artificial world that we have made for ourselves, we create complex problems to which the solutions are often decades away, if solvable at all. In the process of becoming *consumers,* much of our modern society has grossly failed to embrace their role as *producers* of the very things that we consume, things that we rely on the natural world of creation for. Thus, the ever-growing recognition of how important it is to be responsible caretakers and stewards of our natural, renewable resources continues to awaken. Humanity is realizing more than ever that we *need* nature…for many different reasons.

This *need* for nature fills a void within us. It teaches and reminds us of things we often forget or overlook. Nature can heal us and cure the chaos of our hyperactive culture. Beyond the stink of exhaust fumes, and the wretchedness of urban noise pollution, is an oasis of sacred solitude which we all long for. Far removed from the eye-straining abrasion of computer monitors and big-screen televisions lies a sanctuary of soothing, natural stimuli that brings healing and tranquility, rather than exploited turmoil and brain-numbing nonsense. Where the ring of cell phones, non-stop commuting, Pavlovian salivation, and the pavement ends, a primordial universe still remains and beckons us with an irresistible siren song. Although the "pursuit of happiness" in the age of instant information and gratification has transformed many of us into aliens on our own planet, radically unfamiliar with the reality of our natural environment, and truly ignorant in the ways of living in and off the bounty of the earth, we all still long for a deeper connection to creation. In doing so, we can (and should,) *naturally* come to a deeper connection with the Creator.

Caring for Creation

At the heart of this connection between the Creator and creation is embedded our divinely given role of environmental stewards. While people of religious faith gain an awareness of this responsibility through Divine revelation, Sacred Tradition, and Sacred Scripture, even those who are agnostic or atheist still *instinctively recognize* this responsibility as well, though in obviously different ways. Indeed, just as all of humanity *instinctively recognizes* the beauty and goodness of creation, all of humanity *instinctively recognizes* that we, in turn, should be good to it and that we should treat the earth with great respect, care, and even devotion. We *intuitively recognize* the evil of abusing it. By means of spending quality time in nature, we come to *automatically know* that we are not just mere animals, designed to roam the land, and carelessly, selfishly, gobble up and destroy whatever resources are available for our mere survival, even though many people, unfortunately, do just that.

While common sense, logic, and basic intelligence tell us that we must be responsible stewards of the earth, simply in order to continue to live and thrive on it, expressing great care for creation and even possessing a love of it, is something that goes much deeper than a mere animalistic survival instinct. Just as recognizing that the incredible beauty of nature brings forth a spiritual response from us, I propose that the desire to care for that beauty is more of a spiritual dynamic, and not purely one of the intellect. Religion (of various traditions) teaches that human beings are made in the "image and likeness of God," and that we are made by a loving God, out of love, for the purpose to love. Along with that, we also share in the creative powers of God. We are able to bring new life into the world, give birth to ideas, as well as creating material things by means of our mind and body. I have no doubt that this love and creativity, which is embedded in the core of our being, is where our desire to love and care for creation flows. However, actualizing that desire is where common sense, logic, and intelligence must then step in.

This divinely charged responsibility to be guardians and caretakers of nature is a particular area where science and religion work beautifully together. Proper stewardship of the earth cannot be attained through emotion-driven, subjective, radically misinformed avenues of "environmental activism," as is often the case. Nor can it be attained through purely religious, spiritual, or philosophical ideology. Rather, implementing responsible stewardship becomes the objective, diligent work of wildlife biologists, conservationists, natural resource experts and other professionals who are at the front lines. It is their task to *create* sound, scientifically verifiable applications that will ensure proper management of our natural, renewable resources for generations to come. From the objective data that science gives us about nature and how to care for it properly, all of humanity can then join in and properly carry out their divinely given role as stewards of creation, and do so with great love and devotion. Rest assured, when our work is done properly, humanity as a whole can stand back and proclaim with tremendous awe and wonder, "Oh, my God! Look at that!"

(Photograph locations: Twin Lakes, Eagle River, and Kodiak Island, Alaska.)

CHAPTER 3
HELL ON EARTH

Have I entered hell? I write these words on a miserable summer night. I'm camped out with borrowed gear near the Karluk River in a bug and bear-infested Alaskan jungle. I'm hunkered down in a leaky tent that has no floor, other than a small tarp that I duct-taped in place. The rain is pouring, as it has been all day. The undersized sleeping bag and mat that I'm using provides little comfort from the uneven terrain and exposed tree roots that my tent is pitched upon. It was the only semi-flat, camp-able spot that I could find for miles around. Though I've been trying to sleep for hours, here I am, wide awake, cold, damp, sun and wind burned from the previous weeks spent being exposed to the elements. I'm covered with insect bites and smelly campfire smoke from the rotting driftwood I've been burning to stay warm, cook my food, and dry out my clothes.

The hat-sized track of a Kodiak brown bear along a trail leading to the Karluk River.

I have not heard the voice of a friend for a long time now. I've been sustaining myself on a steady diet of fish, fat, salt, caffeine and carbs. Though my will has become stronger, my body has become weak and thin. I am dead-dog tired, dirty as can be, stinking, hairy, and sore all over. The few possessions that I have with me are taking a beating and wearing down fast. Every day something breaks. The half-ton bears that roam around don't alarm me one bit. They've become accustomed to my presence, and I to theirs. I'm too exhausted to even think about it all.

Yet, while I sulk in the misery of another prolonged chastising from Mother Nature, the songbirds still sing all around me. Wind-beaten and soaking wet, their sweet, hypnotic melody continues. They belong here…always. They were born here in the wild, and that is where they will die. In this vast, remote land, perhaps I'm the only two-legged creature that has heard their particular song.

As much as I love this rugged wilderness, and often call it home for long expanses of time, the truth is that it is *not* my home, and it will never be. Sometimes, it feels like more of a hell, devoid of, and rejecting, any semblance of love. Even the men and women of modern-day who have strived to *force* an existence for themselves in truly wild places such as this, ultimately have had to rely on those in the "civilized" world to do so.

A Kodiak brown bear charging a pool of salmon.

The Incarnate Wisdom of the Wilderness

The vast wilderness surrounding the Karluk River.

Although I write these words in misery, someday soon, I'll look back and smile. I'll even long for the euphoric discomfort of this moment, and no doubt, I'll return again for more. While I realize that the wilderness is not, and will never be my true home, it is forever a sacred sanctuary, a place of learning, a school of discipline, as well as a temple of worship. I come here to encounter the Creator…to worship and talk to God, and to listen patiently for the answer. I enter this domain of tooth, fang, and claw, to be more aware of my awareness, to remember things I have forgotten, and to revisit the highlighted texts of my previous years. This is where life returns to its simplest elements, to the daily dynamics of living: attaining shelter, water, fire, and food. In some cases, they come easily. In others, one might die first. If you can master the attaining of these basic elements, you can master your life. In this place, the raw manifestation of creation is all around me. Books are written here, not read. Even in the midst of storms and great discomfort, these places still fill me with tremendous peace. It is here that I absorb and learn the wisdom that is indeed incarnate all around me. Here I am reminded of what *truly* matters.

What *truly* matters does not matter out here in the wild. The birds care nothing of these words I write. The bears have no idea what I feel inside my soul. The mountains and the trees pay no attention and offer no empathy in regard to my dreams and desires, trials and tribulations, or anything else for that matter. Long after I'm gone, the sun will rise and set just the same. The creation that I love will one day gladly consume the very flesh from my bones, with no sympathy for my departure. With or without me, the flowers will continue to bloom and the birds will still sing so sweetly. Nature is indifferent to my coming or going and my living or dying. She simply asks (and needs) my reverent respect while I spend time and pass through her domain.

In these times that I live like an animal, I am harshly reminded that I am *not* one, I will never be, and I don't want to be one. As these spiders crawl all over me while I lie here in the dirt, and hordes of bloodthirsty mosquitoes and black flies torment me without end, I find myself longing for the things that are not here. Nowhere here is the love of another. In this cold, wild place, there is no warmth of family or the welcoming smile of a friend. One's humanity becomes dull in the void of human contact. Joy is not as joyful when there is no one to share it with. Beauty is not as beautiful when it is seen alone. Peace is not as peaceful when a soul becomes as restless as the howling wind. Compassion is not as compassionate when the stomach growls and the throat is parched like the desert sand. Tolerance does not exist when the body pines for essential warmth that slips away so easily. All that matters is sustaining 98 degrees. The wilderness teaches the wisdom of what *truly* matters…fast!

The Wild Relationship

Make no mistake, all of creation is good and essential, but that goodness and those essentials must be approached, applied, and respected in the proper context. Just as medicine can heal a disease, at the same time, if applied to the wrong patient at the wrong time, or in the wrong dosage, it can do much harm. In a similar manner, as the forces of nature often work in ways that we humans perceive as "evil," in reality, those "evil" forces can bring about an abundance of regeneration in the grand scheme of the things, as we will see in a later chapter.

For as long as humankind has wrestled with the notion of God, we have also wrestled with the forces of nature and struggled to survive within them. From the most primitive forms of man to those of our species today, we see an ever-present conflict of both striving to be one with creation, live in harmony with it, and yet tame some of its wildness and wrath, that we might live longer, more comfortable, productive, and civilized lives. From the very start of history, we see that while humans recognized they were *in* the wild world, they were not necessarily designed to be *of* it. Humans instinctually recognized that they were destined for a higher role in the order of creation. Hence, as time went on, through tremendous struggle and strife, through utilizing the resources of creation, through evolving and adapting to the challenges of the ever-changing environment, that higher role was ultimately actualized, though not always with the greatest sense of balance.

From the very dawn of our existence, we human beings have had an appreciation of the beauty and magnificence of nature, but also a fear of what it is capable of if we get in its way, if we approach it in a disrespectful manner or out of the proper context. Mother Nature is both a beauty and a beast, but both sides are ultimately ordered toward the goodness of life. Likewise, our relationship with the natural world is like any other. There are moments of euphoric peace, unbridled joy, and also occasions of great pain, discomfort, and sadness. There are up's and down's, good times and bad times, and everything in between. A true relationship with the natural world is similar to that of a quality relationship that we have with another person. It takes understanding, commitment, patience and self-sacrificing love. That relationship will offer us much, teach us abundantly, and share with us a tremendous amount of beauty. However, take heed, because there will be hardships along the way and paramount rigors to endure. Our relationship with creation and the natural world will not always make us feel good. At times, it will leave us empty. In the end, it will leave us for dead…and rightly so.

Creation alone is not what we seek. Nature is not an end in and of itself, except for *itself*. For humanity, *nature* is a catalyst for things *supernatural*. All the magnificence and incarnate wisdom that the wilderness offers is an outward expression of a hidden reality. Never forget, all of creation points us to the Creator, who *is* what we seek, what we need, what we desire, whether we are consciously aware of it or not. Again, to be made in the "image and likeness of God" is not merely to be a part of creation, to appreciate creation, and exercise powers of creativity ourselves, but rather, to experience and share in the love from which is the very source of creation. This divine love calls us out of the realm of mere creation and invites us to a true, intimate relationship with the Creator, to experience the salvation and redemption that is offered to us, as these are God's greatest works. The revelations of the wild are only signposts to the divine revelation we seek, which is readily available to us. The divine love that the beauty of nature can reveal to us is a true taste of heaven. It pulls us out of what can easily become and ever-beckoning hell.

The revelations of the wild are only signposts to the divine revelation we seek.

CHAPTER 4
TRAILHEAD

*"Stand at the crossroads and look; ask for the ancient paths,
ask where the good way is, and walk in it, and you will find rest for your souls.*
Jeremiah 6:16

For centuries upon centuries, the wilderness has been utilized as a multifaceted place of divine encounter. All the major founders of the world's religions, the primary figures in the Bible, saints, prophets, philosophers, apostles, monks, hermits, and ordinary people of all generations have ventured into the wild for a variety of reasons. Some went to find solace, solitude, inner peace and a greater connection with the sacred. Others journeyed deep into nature to be put to the test, to gain discipline, to go to war with one's inner demons, and to be purified and strengthened in mind, body, and spirit. There are those who have spent time immersed in the wild to learn wisdom, to die to themselves and the world they know, in order that a new one may emerge. Some go to do penance, pray, prepare or study. Others go to experience a sense of "freedom," or at least to find a neutral setting of indifference, and a sense of comfort in living a life on nature's terms, instead of those of the civilized world. No matter what the initial inspiration, those of pure intention walk the path into the wilderness to encounter, and hopefully find, that which is ultimately good, fulfilling, nourishing, liberating, healing, and restorative.

The flip side, however, is that there are also those who enter the wild to seek and carry out dark, dastardly deeds in the secrecy of nature. Murderers, thieves, rapists, and criminals of all kinds have been drawn to the hidden realm of the wilderness in pursuit of terrible atrocity. Just as portrayed in sacred scripture, in the "garden" there is present the opportunity for humanity to engage in both great good and horrific evil. The indifference of the wild is ever-present. In the midst of it, one is faced with many temptations and serious, life-altering choices.

It's precisely because of this indifference found in nature that one discovers the full-force of objective, unfiltered, unforgiving reality, and the need for making strong, conscious decisions while spending time there. Mother Nature does not "spin" the facts, and one's opinion or status is utterly meaningless to her. When harshly faced with either an objectively positive or negative choice, one *must* choose that which is the higher good in order to survive and thrive. When dealing with circumstances that are totally out of one's control, as often happens in the wilderness, one is terminally required to make conscious, willful decisions that promote perseverance, and ultimately, victory over adversity. When one's self is the only human present to witness or judge the morality of one's actions, one is faced with the raw essence of ethical choice. When the sustaining of our life comes down to fulfilling four basic needs (shelter, water, fire, and food) we are fiercely reminded of what is truly essential for life. We realize how fragile and precious it is, and how so much of what we kill ourselves to attain and accomplish during our time in the "world," is laughably unimportant in the grand scheme of things.

While it can be easy to judge this "indifference" of nature as being something "evil," it is, in fact, good and necessary. Just as the "bad," potentially destructive forces of nature can bring about regeneration in the long term, so too, the "bad things" that we experience in the natural world have the potential to bring about tremendous growth in us. Even Jesus, who Christians believe is God incarnate, experienced tremendous temptation and hard choices, as well as the wrath and extreme discomfort of nature, during his time in the wilderness.

A Positive Indifference

The indifference of nature can, and should, greatly inspire us to choose and strive for that which is good. While we are not *forced* to do so, we come to realize quite alarmingly the consequences of making bad choices. Perhaps, one of the most important, truly divine lessons that the wilderness teaches is this one: *We are created for goodness.* Our relationships, the core of who we are as human beings, the power of our will, our ability to make responsible choices, our true freedom, etc., all revolve around and are contingent upon our ability to consciously choose that which is good. As all major religions teach, that which is "good" is that which is of God.

Indeed, there is a tremendous amount to be learned from the Creator through creation. No matter if one is simply spending a few hours, the better part of a weekend, or if one is on a hard-core, extended stay in the wild, lessons *will* be taught and an education *will* be received. Nature has a wonderful way of teaching us what we *need* to learn or experience, not always so much of what we *want* to. The old saying holds true, "Man plans and God laughs."

When one stands at the trailhead, there is an endless world of possibilities that open up. A vast library of knowledge and a gallery of sacred beauty, which goes far beyond the imagination, becomes available. There are challenges that will forge one's will into steel or break it in two. The trail can lead to a life-changing encounter for better or for worse. The choice is ours. We must seek the "good way," and walk in it. Whatever the case, there is no retreating once the feet are in motion on the ancient path. As reminded by the prophet Jeremiah, every step is an opportunity to find rest for the soul. Come and see. A new day is about to dawn!

(Photograph locations: Twin Lakes, and Spruce Island, Alaska.)

CHAPTER 5
LET THERE BE LIGHT

It happens every morning. From an abyss of blackness, a slight glow emerges on the horizon. As the glow intensifies, the silhouettes of clouds appear and slowly become backlit in the expanding light. Shades of primary colors begin to gently brew and blend in the eastern atmosphere. Meanwhile, ever so subtly, the landscape below begins to take shape in the ever-growing illumination of the dawning day. Outlines and evolving distinctions lethargically develop out of the darkness. As the horizon continues to brighten, the surrounding skies begin to absorb the light and reflect it down upon the land, giving it greater clarity and definition with every passing moment.

While the clouds on the horizon remain silhouetted and dark, the atmosphere behind them becomes increasingly brighter. In the east, an epicenter of intense color begins to exert dominance in the sky. A fire slowly burns and impregnates the surrounding clouds with hues of orange and red. A soft pink and yellow glow begins to overtake the horizon and gently evolves into a vastness that blankets the heavens. As the pink and yellow light transforms into red and orange, the outline of surrounding mountains begins to separate themselves from the clouds along the skyline. Meanwhile, the still waters below reflect a mirror image of what is above, creating a perfect earthly harmony.

As the clarity, exposure, and saturation of natural light and color are increased with every second of passing time, the grand finale of earthly awaking rather suddenly reaches a climax and erupts from the stoic stillness of the morning prelude. From the burning eastern epicenter on the horizon, the great universal source of light and heat begins to take a peek upon the land. As the sun fully reveals itself and rises above all of creation, the backlit clouds become a soft blue, and all the colors of the morning masterpiece explode into magnificence and give birth to the new life of day.

Almost instantly, as if on cue from the divine conductor, the world awakens! As the first shadows are cast upon the land, owls begin to hoot, crows cackle, turkeys gobble, bull elk bugle, songbirds joyfully chirp, and every creature on earth joins in a wonderful symphony, grateful that light and warmth has returned to the land.

Living in the Light

In recent times, scientists have linked a host of serious illnesses to vitamin D deficiency. While too much time spent in direct sunlight certainly has risks of its own, the dangers associated with spending too little time are actually far greater. Human beings were designed to be creatures of the light. Even though one can increase the levels of vitamin D in the body through nutrition and artificial supplementation, there is no substitute for the healing and regenerative powers that come from the sun.

Lack of sunlight not only affects the body in negative ways, but perhaps even more so, the mind. Depression, suicide, and self-destructive behavior run rampant in environments where sunlight is minimal, such as the winter climates of the far north. Moods plummet like the mercury of a thermometer in such places. Those who work night shifts for long periods of time, and those who for whatever reason simply don't spend much time in the sun, can also attest to the cumulative negative effects that come from rarely seeing the light of day. One begins to enter a state of mind that is not so pleasant. No matter what the case, darkness can start enveloping the mind and even the soul in the absence of the sun.

There is the potential for great danger in the darkness. One can easily forget how intense it can be, on all levels, whether it's the complete, total pitch black of an overcast night in the wilderness, the darkness of depression, or the darkness that comes from self-destructive behavior. When totally enveloped by darkness of any kind, there is great confusion. An overwhelming paralysis inhibits the sense of direction and produces a fear of the unknown. Dangers remain hidden and predators are camouflaged with blackness and shadow. Startling sounds unsettle the nerves and unexpected movement becomes cause for alarm, panic and even paranoia. Confidence is swallowed up in an abyss of doubt. When light is absent, there is only a desperate, primordial groveling to survive. The essentials of life are groped at blindly. The path is cold and indiscernible.

It's only by means of living in the light that one discovers its liberating power! In the light, one discovers truth. The negative is replaced with positive. Truth transforms the *destructive* into the *constructive*. Worry and fear are cast aside and exposed as the useless parasites they are. Doubts are replaced with hope when illuminated by truth. Light clearly reveals that which was unknown and uncertain, and replaces it with confidence, courage, healing, and a newfound sense of direction. The pathways of both the wilderness and of one's life become welcoming and warm once again. There is great joy that comes when one realizes that what was feared or hidden in darkness only prevented the discovery of life-giving, awe-inspiring beauty!

A Kodiak brown bear soaking in the life-giving warmth and light of the sun.

A Light in the Darkness

While the light of day is a phenomenon that we simply cannot live without in a healthy manner, there is still a light in the darkness that shines forth in the absence of the sun. It is a light that can carry one through the black of night until a new day dawns. It often goes unnoticed and unappreciated. It takes some adjustment, education, and practice to be utilized to its fullest potential. Nevertheless, it is there. It is the light that shines from the heavens at night; the moon, the stars, the planets. They do, in fact, reflect a significant amount of illumination…sometimes a tremendous amount! While the "light pollution" from urban and city environments make it extremely difficult to notice, when out in the remote wilderness on a clear or even partly cloudy night, the light from the sky brightens up everything, even to the point of creating shadows.

It's truly amazing how much light is given off from the atmosphere when the sun goes down. While it's still dark and dangerous, the illumination from the heavens can bring hope to an otherwise unmanageable situation. Again, the moonlit sky can create enough brightness to comfortably make it through the paralyzing darkness of night. The stars can provide a navigable path to safety in the midst of confusion. Not only that, the glowing constellations and aurora borealis are incredibly beautiful sights to behold, a sight that makes one realize how small, but unique, we are in the universe at large.

While nature's "night light" can be of great assistance and give comfort and courage, there is a light in the soul that acts much the same. It is always there, but often goes unnoticed. It can be incredibly useful and powerful, but it is developed and strengthened slowly. It is the light of faith. The virtue of faith is the ability to see in the dark. It is a spiritual "night vision." Just as one can learn to function quite well in low light settings and work with the subtle, but sustainable illumination of the stars to navigate a course at night, faith is the capacity to trust, and work with a force much greater than one's self, instead of working against it. The light of faith enables one to navigate and properly function during times of life that are enveloped by the darkness of doubt. Faith enables one to *trust* in the light of truth, to *know* that it is there, to have total confidence that it will rise up and brighten our path once again.

(Photograph locations: Kodiak Island, Alaska.)

CHAPTER 6
THE ADVENTURE OF ADVENTURE

Getting ready to venture into the wild, for whatever purpose, is an adventure in and of itself. As it's been said, "The journey is the destination." Researching a particular place to explore, making all the preparations, and actually going there to do it, are all exciting and necessary elements of any wilderness adventure. With every piece of gear that is readied and packed, the mind races with excitement of what it will actually be like to use it when the time comes. The pre-adventure planning and prep time is one filled with exhilarating hope and joyful imagination! Speaking personally, as I prepare for time in nature, whether it's a simple day trip or a hardcore, super remote solo excursion, I often feel like a little kid who's anxiously awaiting Christmas. With each passing day leading up to the big shove off date, I'm literally exploding with childlike glee and frenzied anticipation! I just can't wait to get out there and go!

The author on a solo wilderness adventure at Twin Lakes, Alaska.

It's very important, however, not to let all that excitement cloud one's thinking while in the preparation stage, as those preparations must be made with extreme care and hyper-sensitive attention to detail. In addition, it is imperative that one is in constant, extremely thorough communication with the other members of one's group while making preparations. Planning and going over every tiny detail together is a must. If going alone, first be aware that doing a remote, wilderness solo adventure is a serious, high-risk activity and it is certainly not something for beginners. Make sure trusted people know exactly what your plans are and have emergency procedures in place before heading out.

When gearing up for an advanced outdoor adventure, it's important to first do a reality check. Ask yourself, "Am I genuinely, *honestly* ready for this? Am I in good mental and physical shape? Do I have the necessary *tested* skills? Have I done my homework in regard to the area I'll be in? Have I diligently planned for every conceivable scenario of this adventure? Etc., etc.?" One has to approach the wild with ultimate respect! While stories of ill-prepared adventure seekers meeting their demise in the wilderness might make for exciting books and movies, I can tell you from experience that it's not so exciting when it's you or your friend who is about to die!

The remote wilderness is no place to fool around or do things half-heartedly. Hospitals, medical assistance, and help of any kind are often miles and even days away. Even with emergency devices such as a satellite phone or EPIRB, (emergency position indicating radio beacon) help can still be next to impossible. If the weather turns south, which you can expect, forget about anyone flying in to rescue you. You're simply food for the wolves and bears.

One must make every conceivable preparation to stay safe on wilderness adventures. In most cases, the only helping hands out there are at the end of your arms. Make a gear list well in advance, based on your research of the area you are going into, and then check, recheck and quadruple check your preparations before heading out. Also, keep in mind, that if you are being flown into the wilderness, one is limited to around 100 to 150 pounds of gear for most fights on a bush plane. So, what you pack has to be light, absolutely essential, simple, dependable, and as multi-purpose as possible. This is no time to forget anything!

A floatplane is often the only way in or out of the remote wilderness.

Lapses of memory or blundering oversights simply **cannot** be a part of preparing for remote adventures. Your life may depend on what you happened to forget, and while knowing how to *improvise, adapt and overcome* is of the greatest importance and certainly comes into play at times, there is just no way out of certain situations without the proper gear, period. For example, if you wear contacts and/or glasses and absolutely depend on them, you had better bring an extra set or two with you. I've seen some incredible bush craft over the years, but have yet to see someone make wearable prescription lenses from a chunk of ice. And, if you rely on medications of one kind or another, again, take plenty of extra and keep them in separate places so you have a backup. Don't keep all your eggs in one basket, as they say.

In gearing up for serious outdoor adventure, it is imperative to do your homework well in advance regarding the actual location you will be in. Get quality, up to date maps, study the topography and the available natural resources that are in the area for shelter, water, fire, and food. If there are discernible, useable game or people trails…or at least obvious potential travel routes in the area…become familiar with them, and USE THEM! Trying to bushwhack your own path through the uncharted wilderness can be an exhausting, dangerous, frivolous ordeal that will get you nowhere in a hurry…except maybe dead! Also, while high tech gadgetry like GPS units and smartphones can come in handy, never trust your safety and overall wellbeing to things that run on batteries. The skill sets that one relies on in the wilderness must be embedded in one's brain and accessible through one's hands…not in an electronic box. Be well aware of the weather extremes that you might encounter, because you will probably experience at least some of them. Be well prepared to deal with pests, both big and small, from hungry, camp raiding bears to hordes of pesky insects that materialize when least expected. A simple bug head net is worth its weight in gold!

Lecturing like a worrisome mother, I could go on and on with more, but the bottom line here is that one must be *extremely* prepared for *extreme* adventure. There are lots of resources out there to learn more, but the important thing is to practice what you learn. Make it a point to field test your knowledge and skills in areas that will not kill you if you make a mistake. As expert survivalists will tell you, one of the key concepts here is to "Do more with less, because the more you know, the less you need." Indeed, there is great freedom in not *wanting* or *needing* unnecessary things. This is a principle that not only enhances one's time in the field, but more so, it can revolutionize one's life!

The Natural High

A brilliant sunset over the Colorado Rocky Mountains.

The late, great John Denver wrote a hit song entitled, *Rocky Mountain High*, which was criticized by some as being a reference to illegal drug use. For those who have spent quality time in "high places," such as the alpine regions of towering mountain ranges, it becomes quite clear that Mr. Denver was not singing of drug-induced euphoria, but rather that of the bliss that comes from being in mind-blowingly beautiful places in nature. The whole point of making such diligent preparations for remote outdoor adventure is so one can then enjoy that adventure to the absolute fullest without worry, as that is the whole point of it all!

As a personal example, when I head out to the wilderness for an extended nature or wildlife photography trip, I prayerfully invite the Spirit of God to lead me, as my photography work has always been a means of capturing moments in which God has revealed something to me through incredible experiences of his creation. After I set up my camp, get everything in order and fully orient myself, I simply grab my pack of diligently prepared essential gear; pick a direction or geographical feature that inspires me the most at the moment, and go!

As I begin a journey through the wilds, the journey, indeed, becomes the destination itself. I move very slowly and carefully with each step, not just to be cautious of the terrain, but more so, to keep my eyes open and be fully aware of my surroundings. I focus intently on everything from grand, mountain vistas, to the tiniest insect on the ground. Keep in mind, the most important piece of equipment that a photographer has is his or her eyes! The best camera equipment in the world is utterly worthless if one does not have a trained, disciplined eye to seek out beauty, recognize it in overlooked places, and learn to instinctively predict where it will materialize. I often see people with cameras rushing down nature trails as if in a race, meanwhile, passing right by so many incredible photographic opportunities. Sloooooow Doooooown!

Slowing down is not only essential for developing "the eye," and fully exercising one's powers of awareness, but more so, it's extremely therapeutic. While some gravitate towards various forms of prayer and meditation that are stationary, or rather sedentary in practice, there is nothing that clears the mind and places one in the totality of God's loving presence quite like going for a walk in the wild, in the cathedral of creation! Walking can become contemplative prayer in motion. An explorational nature walk can completely clear the head of all the worldly clutter that can collect in one's mind over the months. One is reconnected to the Creator as he or she travels the paths that have been made by God's creation…either man or beast. And along with the spiritual and mental cleansing that takes place, walking also purifies the body by getting the blood flowing and the oxygen stirring; it stimulates, as well as relaxes, the muscular tensions that create stress and can take a toll on one's self over time.

Going on prayerful walks in the wilderness transforms one into a kind of sponge, soaking up the love, the peace, and the glory of God with heartfelt gratitude. One doesn't have to utilize a particular method of prayer on such walks, but rather, just go and humbly listen to the Lord, praising and thanking God for all that is seen, heard, smelled, felt, tasted and touched…realizing how incredibly blessed one is to behold such wonder. The sensory experience of taking in the beauty of creation while in motion becomes a catalyst for being united with the omnipotent presence of the Creator. With the Spirit of God present, and being consciously connected to that Spirit, the *natural* becomes the *supernatural* once again.

Walking in high places does wonders for the mind, body, and soul.

Back Down to Earth

While all this spiritual, inspirational stuff might sound great, the reality of going on long treks in areas of remote wilderness, along with camping out there, can be a great challenge. Hiking for miles on end through tough terrain, while taking a severe beating from Mother Nature, is not an easy thing to do. Just as with life in general, one has to face those challenges one step at a time, one phase at a time, always striving for a sense of balance, resting when needed, and remaining hopeful, having a positive, optimistic outlook, and ultimately having the faith and the discipline to carry on.

There have been times in the wilderness that I have been totally overwhelmed and utterly intimidated by the challenge of reaching a particular location, surviving in severe weather conditions, or camping in potentially dangerous areas. In such times, one has to again slow down, stay calm, and take things one day, one minute, one task at a time, dividing monumental challenges into small, do-able portions, reaching big goals by accomplishing small ones. Along with that, I can't stress enough the power of staying positive in the midst of it all.

As a final nugget of wisdom, learned the hard way, keep in mind that *fear* is what often prevents one from discovering incredible beauty. I mentioned this previously, but it's worth repeating. Some of my best photographs and most unforgettable experiences in wild nature have come as a result of venturing into areas that I was initially scared to death of, or at least extremely hesitant about. Overcoming fear with the power of knowledge, a little extra courage, and a strong faith, can open up doors to some of the most beautiful, life-changing experiences this side of heaven. The alternative is simply to be paralyzed by the power of fear and live a life of bitter regret. Indeed, the choice is yours!

The journey is the destination!

(Photograph locations: Clearwater Idaho, Snowmass Colorado, Katmai, Twin Lakes, Kodiak Island, Alaska.)

CHAPTER 7
BECOME WATER

There is a scene in the movie *A River Runs Through It,* where a father and his two young sons go out for a day of trout fishing. Upon their arrival at a pristine, Montana river, the father takes a few moments beside the riverbank to describe the process of creation to his sons. As the water gently babbles over the rocks with a peaceful flow, he speaks of it as "The words of God." The scene ends with the three of them listening intently to those immortal words of creation as heard in the tranquility of a mountain stream.

Yes, there is something divine about the sound of moving water, whether it's the trickling of a mountain stream, the soothing crash of ocean waves, or the hypnotic sound of falling rain. Water not only purifies, transforms, and nourishes the earth, but likewise the soul.

Some of the fondest memories of my youth are those spent exploring the nearby rivers and creeks of my hometown. At a very young age, I was powerfully drawn to those places of relative solitude, as if beckoned by a mysterious siren song. Being outside, walking through the woods and along the river banks affected me in a way I couldn't explain. As I admired the festival of life that was going on all around me, it filled my boyhood heart with an uncontainable joy and an infectious spirit of adventure! The thrill and excitement of seeing what was beyond the next river bend, or what kind of creatures were living in and around a particular creek, never got tiring, but only became more and more enriching. Those hours spent exploring nature nurtured my soul and produced within me an unquenchable thirst to get to know the one who was responsible for creating all the wonders that I was experiencing. That thirst is what planted the seeds of spirituality, which later gave birth to a true relationship with God. Creation was a powerful, initial catalyst for coming to know, love, and serve the Creator, as is meant to be.

Throughout my life, I've spent countless hours along rivers, both big and small, ponds and lakes, and the ocean. As a result, I've witnessed their vital role in creation time and time again. They are the lifelines and main arteries that run through the heart of the earth. Every creature that walks and crawls, runs and swims, slithers and flies, depends on water to be refreshed, nourished, and renewed. Water is one of the main ingredients used to make everything in creation. Without it, our world and ourselves would simply dry up and fade away. Water equals life.

As I mentioned in a previous chapter, when you spend a great deal of time in nature, you develop a relationship with it. This is especially the case with a particular body of water. One discovers that it has a personality all its own. It becomes an intimate friend, who like any other, is subject to both internal and external changes, who displays different moods and temperaments, and who needs to be lovingly cherished as well as highly respected. A body of water can offer great comfort and life-sustaining bounty on one day, and on the next, it might be rather unfriendly, or even hostile. You must take the positive along with what is perceived as the negative, realizing that both sides make it who and what it is, just like a human friend.

There is much to be learned from water. As master martial artist Bruce Lee once said, "Empty your mind, be formless, shapeless, like water. Now you put water into a cup, it becomes the cup, you put water into a bottle, it becomes the bottle, you put it in a teapot, and it becomes the teapot. Water can flow, or it can crash. Become water, my friend."

When someone spends a great deal of time observing the element of water in various forms and manifestations, they discover that it is constantly in the process of overcoming obstacles that affect its ebb and flow. Water adapts quickly to the conditions of the environment that it's in. It can flow gently and peacefully, or blast forth powerfully and assertively when necessary. Water meets challenges head-on. It is aware of the reality of change and transformation and does not fear it, knowing that as the old passes away, something new is created in its place. Essentially, water *goes with the flow*, as it must, and as it is ordered to do by its very nature. In doing so, it remains fresh and full of the vital energy with which it has been endowed. Indeed, "Become water, my friend!"

(Photograph locations: Kodiak Island, Alaska.)

CHAPTER 8
LISTENING

As I write these words, I sit alone along the bank of the Ayakulik River on remote Kodiak Island, Alaska. It's early autumn, and after days of howling winds and nasty weather, there is finally a break. It is sunny, warm, and incredibly still. The river is calm, smooth as glass, reflecting a perfect mirror image of the surroundings. Not even the tiniest blade of grass is moving. It's as if the stillness of the morning has somehow stopped time and frozen the motion of everything. The clouds in the sky do not move. They simply hang there, as if painted on canvas by an artist.

When I close my eyes, however, I am made aware of the illusion of this pause of movement. As I tune in, I hear the soft, distant chirping of songbirds, the calling of a broken covey of ptarmigan, the barking of a family of foxes out in the tundra, the squeaking wings and the swooshing sound of eagles in flight. I can hear the annoying buzz of pesky insects that never seem to halt their torment. With eyes still closed, I can detect the subtle sipping and rising of Dolly Varden as they eat the freshly hatching insects. At the same time, huge Coho salmon splash and writhe about as they spawn in the shallow water. Within myself, I can hear the machine of my body at work, the beating of my heart, the breathing of air, my stomach digesting food, the twitching of my eyelids and the slight creaking of my bodily joints. In the far-off distance is the roaring of two brown bears that are most likely feuding over a prized fishing hole.

From behind me, I now begin hearing the distinct, sloshing, thudding footfalls and heavy breathing of an enormous Kodiak bear approaching the fish-laden pool that is before me. As the volume increases, the swampy footsteps transform into what sounds more like paddling noises. I open my eyes to see the bear now swimming, instead of walking, to his destination upriver. He's right on time. He gives me a rather friendly, curious glance, as he does almost every day, and then continues on his way.

While I continue to relish the morning calm of this ancient wilderness, the sound of my pen on paper seems almost deafening with its abrasive scratching. There are no televisions, computers, phones, or distracting gadgetry of any kind out here. At the moment, it's just me, my thoughts, creation, and my God. Such a setting is both peaceful, but also rather confrontational. In the stillness and lack of self-induced distraction, one is forced to face oneself. There is no escape, no masks to be worn, and no denying the contents of one's heart, mind, and soul that are starved for attention, and desperately need to be recognized. At such times, one is faced with the hard questions of *whom* and *what* one genuinely is, and *who* and *what* one is becoming. The stillness interrogates relentlessly and pounds in the reality of the challenges and issues in one's life that simply *must* be addressed. In the solitude and silence, there is no one to water-down the gravity of those issues. There is no one to soothe the hard truth that we humans often so desperately run and hide from, or keep ourselves too busy, or too entertained to pay attention to. In such primordial, sacred silence, one faces the raw nakedness of one's being. The ego disintegrates and is neutralized by the forces of nature. The wilderness cares nothing of one's status in the "world." What matters are right here, right now, you, and you alone.

Hearing VS Listening

In the wilderness, there is tremendous opportunity to exercise one's ability *to hear*, that is, to sharpen one's powers of detecting and identifying the source and direction of sound. Much more importantly, it's in the silence and nakedness of such settings that one has the priceless opportunity to exercise the ability *to listen*. Listening is the catalyst for discovering truth. When everything else is stripped away, when one overcomes the intimidation and discomfort of silent nothingness, and finally, willfully *chooses* to listen to the voice of divine truth, instead of one's own voice or the voices of others, the potential to experience a radical, positive, liberating transformation occurs. In finally coming to recognize, confront, battle, and claim victory over one's personal demons of deception, the result is an unburdening, purifying metamorphosis that emerges like the morning sun shattering the darkness of night.

As the prophet Elijah from the Old Testament experienced, the voice of God was not found in loud, grandiose, dazzling displays of one kind or another, but rather, in the gentle whisper of silence. (1 Kings 19:11-13) Spiritual masters of all generations have experienced this phenomenon. Saint Mother Teresa of Calcutta once said, "We need to find God, and He cannot be found in noise and restlessness. God is the friend of silence. See how nature, trees, flowers, grass, all grow in silence. See the stars, the moon and the sun; how they move in silence. We need silence to be able to touch souls." On another occasion, she stated, "In the silence of the heart, God speaks. If you face God in prayer and silence, God will speak to you. Then you will know that you are nothing. It is only when you realize your nothingness, your emptiness, that God can fill you with Himself. Souls of prayer are souls of great silence."

When it's all said and done, perhaps the Psalmist from the Old Testament summed it up perfectly in writing, "Be still, and know that I am God." (Psalm 46:10) Are you listening?

(Photograph locations: The Ayakulik River of Kodiak Island, Alaska.)

CHAPTER 9
CYCLE OF LIFE

No one gets out alive. Every living thing will pass away. Whether we like it or not, an undeniable reality of living on planet earth is that something must die, (animal or plant,) for something else to live. Unless one eats and lives in dirt, one will be responsible, in one way or another, for the killing and utilizing of other living things. This is a principle that applies to every creature on earth, most especially human beings. While there are immense beauty and vitality in nature, there is of course great savagery and death displayed in the cycle of life. The natural world is not a Disney movie where animals dance together in the forest, share a cup of delightful tea, and exchange pleasantries in a state of global utopia.

The objective, undeniable reality is that all of creation kills and eats other forms of creation, and most do so in ways that humankind would describe as "horrific and brutal." All creatures sustain themselves by searching for (hunting), killing, and eating once living (and feeling) forms of life. The majority of birds, fish, reptiles, amphibians, mammals and even insects, eat other fish, birds, reptiles, amphibians, insects and mammals. The ones that do not (herbivores) become food for the others. While humans are often the cause of the unnecessary killing and suffering of animals, the truth is if there were not one human being on earth, animals would still suffer terribly as a result of other animals struggling for survival, environmental patterns that limit food, unsubstantial water supply, and changing habitats. Again, the wilderness is not Disney, but rather a place of indifference to the death of its inhabitants. At the same time, life goes on, and indeed, it does!

It must always be remembered that the rather harsh realities of nature and the processes that seem mercilessly destructive, are the same ones that ultimately bring about a renewal of life in the grand scheme of things. Consider the thousands upon thousands of salmon that travel hundreds of miles, experience incredible adversity in the process, and upon the completion of their aquatic pilgrimage, they spawn and then die. However, even after this massive display of death, as millions of fish carcasses lie rotting on the banks of rivers, filling the air with a pungent stink, this becomes an absolutely essential source of vitality. The nutrients from the expired fish flow into the water and nourish their offspring as they begin to emerge…thus keeping the cycle of life going strong. Not to mention, the spawning fish also provide food for countless other creatures in the area.

Consider the aftermath of a violent storm. As turbulent winds, crashing waves, flooding waters, scouring rains, and all manner of natural chaos seemingly punish the land and all that dwells upon it, and in fact do claim the lives of many living things, when calm and stability return to the environment, there is ultimately renewal and purification. Raging tides and killer waves blast away the filth, garbage and natural debris that has littered the outskirts of an area. When floodwaters subside, the ground is recharged with vital nutrients. New channels and underwater structures are created, and old obstacles are removed.

Acknowledge, if you will, the aftermath of a hellish, terrifying wildfire. When the flames are extinguished and the smoke clears, the forest floor is cleared and cleaned. Obstructive brush, non-native species of vegetation and weaker or diseased tree/plant life are removed. The result of wildfire allows more nourishment to absorb into the soil and sunlight to penetrate the area. Habitat is improved for wildlife. Grasses and vegetation that animals feed on are greatly regenerated and the water supply is increased. Fire kills the insects and disease that ravages plant and tree life. In fact, studies have shown that many species of plants and trees in nature are actually dependent on fire for the life of a forest to continue.

Awakenings in the Wild

Again, what human beings often consider "evil" or "bad" in the natural world is in many cases actually a designed process that is good and necessary. The powers of nature act much like a dishwashing machine. A cacophony of extreme heat, water, pneumatic forces, etc., all mix together to scour and scrub and ultimately produce sparkling clean, sanitized, purified plates, pots, and pans. A bold, revitalization occurs. A resurrection takes place.

Get Busy Living

One of my favorite movie quotes of all time is from the film, *Shawshank Redemption*. As a falsely accused, imprisoned inmate comes to grip with the reality of forever being behind bars, he comes to a point where he willfully, consciously makes the decision to plan and carry out his justified deliverance. As the process of his redemption begins, he utters the words of his newfound *modus operandi* to a trusted friend, "Get busy living, or get busy dying."

An important, revolutionizing principle to adhere to both in the wilderness and in life is something a wise woman told me many years ago, *"You are in charge of what makes you miserable."* We all must make the choice daily to get busy either living, or dying. While suffering and dealing with "bad things," disasters, and setbacks are simply a part of our earthly experiences that we cannot control, how we *choose* to react to them *is* in our power. We can *choose* to let a difficult situation or negative set of circumstances beat us down and kill our spirit, or we can *choose* to rise to the challenge and grow wiser and stronger by overcoming, or at least positively coping, with those sufferings.

While there is a cycle of life constantly at work in nature, perhaps even more so, there is one going on within the human soul. As I've heard it said, there is a "creative disintegration" that takes place when the core of our being is torn asunder by the storms of life. From the rubble emerges the potential for a new creation within us. Enduring tremendous suffering, out of love, channeled by faith and hope, is that which does bring about a newfound purpose, power, and a vitality from what would otherwise simply be destruction and doom. When a part of us dies, another part comes to life.

We must keep in mind, however, that the negative forces and experiences that we define as "suffering," can only bring about enlightenment and renewal in our cycle of life if we allow it and willfully *choose* it. Just as a wildlife burns away pestilence and regenerates a forest, it's often only by means of the *fire* of suffering that we are *forced* to open our eyes and recognize the things we have been ignoring or taking for granted. Storms of suffering are often the only thing that *forces* open our deaf ears to hear the voice of truth clearly. Suffering teaches appreciation, gratitude, humility, priority, and wisdom with an unmatched intensity. In the midst of unmanageable pain, we finally see through the deceptive illusion of control, which seeks to rule our lives. We cannot *control* the cycle of life, either in nature or within ourselves. We can only recognize the reality of it, and either *willingly*, or *unwillingly* be a part of it. Again, the choice is ours. Either way, we must get busy.

(Photograph locations: Clearwater Idaho, Twin Lakes, Kodiak Island, Alaska.)

CHAPTER 10
OPEN YOUR EYES

There is a big difference between merely having *vision* and exercising our ability to *see*, just as there is a tremendous difference between the ability to *hear* and the act of *listening*, as we reflected on in an earlier chapter. *Vision* is simply possessing the sensory power of sight, while *seeing* is the ability to harness and focus that power to seek out particular objects, minuscule details and gather information that would otherwise go unrecognized and unknown.

You see, we often do not see. We take many things for granted and glance over vast amounts of information in the blink of an eye. Everything we see tells a story and can lead to a new discovery. This is especially true in nature. A fun activity to engage in while in the woods is that of looking for and studying the tracks and "sign" of wildlife. With a little practice, one can learn to recognize easily what animals have visited a particular area. With *a lot* of practice, one can ascertain a tremendous amount of information from a mere animal track.

Professional, master trackers can study a track and tell if the animal was male or female. They can determine whether it had any injuries, exactly what time of day or night it came by, if it was hungry, pregnant, nervous, calm, moving fast or slow, where it was headed, if it stopped to look right or left, up, down, or paused to get a drink. Master trackers exercise mind-blowing attention to detail and pay attention to the most intricate, tiniest characteristics of animal sign.

They harness their awareness and power of vision to go far beyond just looking at the ground. They are *truly* able to *see* as few others can.

While most people don't have the time or the interest to spend countless hours studying the dirt in order to become a master tracker, there is a great lesson to be learned nonetheless. That is the importance of expanding one's awareness, of exercising one's ability to genuinely see. In doing so, a completely new world begins to emerge. In the day and age of big-screen televisions, many have a natural tendency to "see big," to view the world as a huge, high definition, widescreen. This tendency carries over to time spent in the natural world as well. Many people instinctively search out grand, mountain vista overlooks, and massive expanses of scenery where one can take in miles upon miles of wilderness in a single glance. Meanwhile, incredible amounts of beauty go totally unnoticed.

Learning to *see small* goes against the grain of our *think big* society. But in doing so, again, a whole new universe opens up. Taking the time to see and appreciate things like the hand-painted décor of a tiny frog or butterfly, the delicate structure of a hidden wildflower or spider web, the amazing formation of ice crystals, and countless other subjects, makes one realize the immense amount of artistry that is present in creation. Much of which is trampled underfoot or carelessly passed by.

The key to developing a greater sense of awareness in the wilderness and learning to see and appreciate the beauty of the "microworld" of nature is to *sloooooow down...way down!* As I mentioned earlier, vast amounts of information and spectacular displays of natural wonder are so often totally unnoticed, because of being in a huge rush, which is another habit ingrained in us by our fast-paced, high-speed culture. As a rule of thumb, if while walking down a trail you constantly find yourself watching your step and scanning the ground for obstacles in your way, then you are going way too fast, unless your goal is simply to do a trail run for some exercise.

Exploring the micro world of nature means to take the time to do just that...explore! It's great fun to recapture that childlike sense of adventure and discovery by turning over rocks to see what is under them, crawling around in the dirt and mud looking at the tiny, camouflaged creatures that live there, sneaking up on a feeding butterfly or trying not to scare away a sunbathing lizard. Not only is it fun, but it's also very challenging!

Of course, not only are these principles applicable to appreciating nature more, but more importantly, they apply to appreciating our fellow human beings. We often rush through life so fast, with so many distractions, that we overlook the beauty and value of each other. There is a vast universe within each human person, waiting to be shared and discovered. There are so much wonder and awe in a soul that goes unnoticed for various reasons. Sometimes, it can be very hard to see or find. Sometimes, you find it buried deep by time and circumstance, or protected by a hard, protective shell, but the love and the beauty with which we all were initially created is indeed there. One simply needs to *sloooow* down in order to recognize it, and patiently exercise the ability to truly see.

(Photograph locations: Kodiak Island, Alaska, Ava, Missouri.)

CHAPTER 11
WILD FREEDOM

There are few things as majestic as witnessing an eagle in flight, soaring high through rugged mountain passes and gliding over calm waters as a new day dawns. The ability to fly seemingly defies worldly constraints and the very law of gravity which holds everything to the earth. The eagle goes where it chooses, effortlessly passing over barriers and obstacles of all kinds. For Americans, especially, this mighty raptor embodies the freedom we hold so dear, constantly strive for, and will fight to the death to protect.

While the majestic bald eagle, and other birds of prey, symbolize all that is wild, free, and regal, the reality of their existence is something quite different from what most imagine. In truth, the eagle's life is not so liberated, but rather, it is one of harsh survival and enslavement to the cycles of nature. During the summer months in places like coastal Alaska, eagles thrive and feast like kings on an unlimited supply of protein-rich salmon, which they gorge themselves on daily. However, as summer turns to winter and the last of the spawning fish die and disappear, the eagles become homeless nomads, traveling the trail of blood, desperately searching for the next meal, no matter how small or unpalatable.

A young bald eagle perched on top the backbone of a whale carcass.

As the land becomes snow-covered and desolate, these magnificent birds will gather around dumpsters and parking lots, fighting over tidbits of filthy trash. They will line up like pigeons on the rooftops of fish processing plants, waiting for hours to prey upon a single rotten scrap. They will engage in savage, violent battles over those few available scraps. Seeing bloody, injured, or even dead eagles in such areas is common. If an eagle is lucky enough to find a road-killed animal, it will plunge its resplendent white head into the body cavity and consume the carcass with fervor, slinging gore and entrails about in a desperate display. When the day is done, our national birds will roost on protected hillsides and alder thickets, doing their best to lessen the merciless, assaulting blows from Mother Nature that come during a brutal winter night.

When considering these details, the eagle does seem to be the perfect representative of our nation, as it symbolizes, and truly experiences, the same realities of the people of our country. While there are those who hoard the benefits of our nation's "freedoms" and greedily revel in a lavish, selfish, irresponsible lifestyle, there are also those who have endured hell on earth in order to survive and thrive. They are the ones that genuinely exercise freedom, who know its true nature, who will fight to protect it, and who cherish it with the highest gratitude.

Natural Freedom

During the last half-century or so, modern society has in many cases completely reversed and manipulated the true meaning of freedom, and replaced it with a philosophy of greed and hedonism…a way of life focused on attaining selfish pleasure at any cost with no regard for personal responsibility or the consequences of one's actions. Choosing to embrace ideologies and engage in activities that are extremely unhealthy and destructive, both physically and emotionally, individually and societally, is not an act of liberation or an expression of one's freedom, but rather one of enslavement and degradation.

It's interesting to note that in the writings of the world's greatest leaders, as well as the texts of spiritual masters from various traditions, whenever the word "liberation" or "freedom" is used, it is in reference to things that are evil. Likewise, stories from sacred scripture speak of *freedom* from immorality, of being *liberated* from the captivity of vice, slavery, persecution, death, etc. In a similar manner, when someone is healed of a serious illness, they joyfully proclaim that they are *free* from the disease. When an addict once and for all breaks the chains of their addiction, they heroically claim victory over that which bound them for so long. True freedom is about being *free* from things that are unhealthy, unholy, destructive, negative, and enslaving. Freedom is possessing and exercising the ability to consciously choose what is good, constructive, healthy, and life-giving, while responsibly, willfully rejecting that which is not.

The wilderness is often thought of as the place of ultimate, wild freedom, and again, the mighty eagle personifies that notion. In reality, the wilderness in and of itself is not a euphoric domain of freedom, but rather that of indifference, where both immense beauty and horrific atrocity simultaneously occur. However, as discussed earlier, true freedom *can* be found in nature, and it *must* if one is to survive there. Like the mighty eagle, or every other creature that lives in the wild, human beings especially, *must* consciously choose that which is constructive, positive, and good in order to survive and thrive. The ability to make willful, conscious, responsible, life-giving decisions is what defines the true essence of freedom; the freedom that nature offers, and the freedom for which we strive.

(Photograph locations: Kodiak Island, Alaska.)

CHAPTER 12
RIGHT NOW

Encountering an elusive animal in the wilderness is one of the most memorable and exhilarating experiences that one can hope for while traveling the trails of nature. The moment one locks eyes with a wary, wild creature is simply amazing! At first, there is a reaction of surprise, for both human and animal, followed by a quick, identifying study of the other, and finally, recognition and eventual fleeing. While most humans enjoy seeking out safe experiences of wildlife in their natural habitat, most wild creatures, on the other hand, want nothing to do with humans…unless there is food involved.

An animal definitely knows when people have invaded its home, even if just to pass through respectfully. The sensory powers and level of awareness that wildlife possess far surpasses that of humans. A deer, for example, can smell you and detect your presence in the woods long before you ever set foot on the trail. The rather noisy, fast-paced footsteps and bodily movements of most individuals act as a resounding intruder alert to every creature in the area.

Nevertheless, with great care, forethought, and the development of stealth skills, one can go undetected for much longer periods of time, thus, increasing the odds of a cherished wildlife encounter.

There is indeed something magical about viewing animals in wild nature. Seeing a mother tenderly caring for her young warms even the coldest heart. Watching juvenile creatures play and practice their instinctive skills together fills one with a fun-loving wonder. Being in the proximity of a large, extremely powerful and potentially dangerous beast summons forth instant, overwhelming respect and caution. Admiring the graceful movements, the agility, and the speed of certain animals can be comparable to witnessing a well-rehearsed ballet.

Recognizing the reality of what wild creatures must endure to survive brutal winters, constant predatory attacks, and unimaginable harsh climates, commands the highest level of appreciation and even great sympathy. When that magical moment of locking eyes with such a creature occurs, one can see the intensity of the survival instinct and a desperate longing for life…if just for one more day. Wild animals have within them an immediacy of life that most humans will never be fully able to comprehend, especially while living in a culture in which instant gratification and comfort are considered the highest goods.

If there is one thing for certain that a wild animal can teach a human being, it's the importance of making the most of each moment of life, of living life to the fullest in the present tense, not in the past, not in the future, but in the *now*. While mistakes of the past are a vital source of education for an animal, those mistakes and negative experiences are not dwelled upon obsessively. *Now* is all an animal has. *Now* is all humans have as well. Living in the *now,* as human beings, must not be done so in a hedonistic manner, in which one is only concerned about one's immediate pleasure. Rather, truly living in the *now* is a way of life that makes the most of the present moment as a way of responsibly ensuring the most for the future.

As quality time spent in the wilderness can remind one, it can be so easy to be haunted by the mistakes and tribulations of the past, or worry oneself silly about the future, so much so, that one can completely overlook and grossly fail to appreciate the gift of life that is today. It's so incredibly easy to fail to live in the *now*…to be the best human being, child of God, mom, dad, sibling, son, daughter, etc., that one can be right now. It's so easy to take for granted the beauty and blessings that our eyes, ears, and hearts behold each and every day, so easy to take for granted the air we breathe, the health of our bodies, our relationships, and the many, many priceless blessings from God that we ignore…until they are gone.

In our fast-paced society, we tend to rush through life with such blinding speed that indeed, we do become blind. We become blind to the pricelessness of *today*, hoping that *tomorrow* will bring what we seek, that the *future* holds the realization of our dreams and plans. While that might be the case to varying degrees, tomorrow also might never come, or when it does arrive, we might not be of sound body and mind to enjoy it. The only thing that the future holds for us here on earth with total certainty is our death, which we often sprint toward with incredible, unconscious haste.

Stop! Sloooow down! Appreciate each step you take on the path of life. Take the time to "smell the roses" as they say. Enjoy their sweet fragrance and delicate beauty while you are alive and well, not when they will decorate your grave, or the grave of someone you never took the time to love and appreciate while they were alive. Now is the time!

(Photograph locations: Kodiak Island, Portage, Alaska, Ava Missouri.)

CHAPTER 13
FROM THE WILDERNESS TO THE WORLD

As I described at the beginning of this book, there have been many individuals who have ventured into the wilderness for various reasons throughout the centuries. For most, especially those of our modern-day, a stay in the wild is relatively short term. Thus, there has always been fascination and intrigue with those who trade the "world" for the wilderness for extended periods of time, or who even make that substitution permanently. Why do such individuals leave everything behind to live a solitary life in nature for weeks, months, or even years? What are they looking for? What do they do out there? Are they running or escaping from something? Are they simply not fit to live in civilized society? The questions keep coming.

The stories of those rare individuals who live such lives of wild seclusion often become the subject matter of books, movies, and modern-day legend. Individuals such as Dick Proenneke and Chris McCandless come to mind. Dick, in his 50s, left the "world" behind, built a little cabin in the Alaskan wilderness and lived the rest of his life there, mostly alone, but very happy and successful, as the word "success" applies to surviving and *truly thriving* while living in nature. Chris, on the other hand, was a young man who also ventured alone into the wilds of Alaska for an extended stay, but due to lack of preparedness and skill, he tragically starved and died there. Both stories have been made into bestselling books and films.

The famous wilderness cabin of Dick Proenneke.

The "magic bus" where Chris McCandless lived and died during his time in the wild. (Photo courtesy of Ron Lamothe.)

It's not often that one gets the opportunity to sit down with such a person and find out what makes them tick, why they chose such a life, and how they actually live it. In the spring of 2008, I was blessed to have such an opportunity. On May 23rd of that year, I found myself taking the long way home from a trip to the Great Smokey Mountains in East Tennessee. Many hours, and hundreds of miles later, I was surrounded by yet another captivating, (though smaller), set of majestic peaks: the Ozark Mountains of Southern Missouri, a place I was quite familiar with and visit often. I didn't take the extra-long, gas-guzzling, more scenic route home just for the enjoyment of it though. I did so in order to keep an appointment which was years in the making.

That particular appointment was with Father Robert Matter, a Trappist monk and priest who has lived much of his life in the solitude of nature as a hermit. It was a unique privilege and a true joy to be able to sit down and visit with such a man. In preparation for our meeting, I composed a list of interview questions, which I hoped would guide our discussion about his rather uncommon lifestyle, and also reveal some of Fr. Robert's wisdom and insights.

I actually met Fr. Robert some fifteen years earlier upon my very first visit to *Assumption Abbey*. I should point out that Assumption Abbey is one of the most remote monasteries in the United States. And, by the way, they make AWESOME fruitcakes! The Abbey grounds consist of well over a thousand acres of rugged wilderness, which is then surrounded by the 1.5 million-acre Mark Twain National Forest. Needless to say, it is a dwelling of vast, wild solitude. At the time I first became acquainted with Fr. Robert, I was participating in a month-long workshop, which was focused on learning more about various styles of spirituality and religious vocations. The first part of the program began with a trip to the Abbey to discover more about monasticism and the distinctive style of a monk's life. During the second day of our stay, a group of seven of us was given the opportunity to visit with Fr. Robert at his hermitage. It was a unique treat that I greatly looked forward to, as he rarely met with the public.

My initial reaction was that this humble, well-aged monk looked like something out of a movie, as he wore a long, impressive-looking white beard from his chiseled face. His countenance was one of focused concentration, gentle piety, and quiet wisdom. He had a very peaceful demeanor about him. That afternoon, Fr. Robert told us briefly about his life and times as a hermit. He mentioned that God chooses some *from* humanity to focus solely on praying and sacrificing *for* humanity, which he believes is at the heart of his vocation and life. As the conversion continued, he gave us an overview of his particular style of spirituality and emphatically reminded us that, "We can't give to others what we don't have," namely, that of the intimate knowledge of God that comes through prayer. As our visit came to a close, he encouraged us to always strive to live a simple life, as he stated, "When we make our lives complex, *we*, (not God), create complex problems which *we* must then solve."

I never forgot that initial encounter with Fr. Robert. Over the years, I found myself reflecting on it often, especially his departing words of wisdom to us that day. In the years that followed, I would see Father very briefly at Sunday Mass with the rest of the monks when I would make my annual visit to the Abbey, but I never had the opportunity to speak with him again until that day in May of 2008. It was something I looked forward to for a long time. It's also an experience that I now especially treasure, as Fr. Matter died on November 10, 2017, at the age of 92.

The Roots of a Wilderness Monk

Fr. Robert Matter at his hermitage on the day of our visit.

Around 12:45 PM on that beautiful spring day, I followed a little hand-drawn map on a letter from Fr. Cyprian, the monk who kindly arranged my visit. I walked up a secluded dirt road to the top of a heavily forested hill, and around the bend was an even more secluded path, which led to Fr. Robert's current hermitage. I wasn't sure if I was in the right place, so I cautiously made my way to the screen door and slowly peeked in as if I were carefully examining a hornet's nest. Looking right back at me through a pair of big plastic reading glasses, with a pleasant smile on his face, was the 82 and a half-year-old Fr. Robert, complete with that great white beard of his, now even longer. He graciously invited me in and we casually chatted as I set up my recording gear. There was a very pleasant, relaxed atmosphere about his hermitage. His humble home was a simple wooden structure with just the bare necessities of life. The only slight disturbance at his residence was the sound of the occasional vehicle passing through the Ozark hills somewhere in the distance.

When all was in order and my recording gear was running, we sat down in some sturdy wooden chairs and began a more detailed, concentrated conversation. The first thing I inquired about was Father's upbringing and his general background. Some of my friends and associates back home that were aware of this upcoming interview were very curious as to what kind of environment a (future) hermit was raised in and came from. Was there some kind of personal tragedy, social deficiency, or profound divine revelation that ultimately drove this man to live a life of extreme solitude in the shadow of a Trappist monastery hidden away in the wilderness of the Ozark Mountains? Time would soon tell.

As I found out, Father was born in 1925 and grew up in a small, rustic area of Minnesota. He had a normal life for a lad of his day and age. As a teenager, he received his high school education in St. Cloud, where his family moved in the fallout of the Great Depression. At the age of 18, Fr. Robert tried to enlist in the Navy, but he was rejected due to a heart murmur. Just a few months later, however, he was drafted. The heart murmur was apparently overlooked that time, and he ended up serving for four years as a corpsman.

During those years in the military, Father noted that he reflected quite a bit on his life and thought seriously about becoming a priest. During his last six months of service, he decided that he was, in fact, being called to a religious vocation. Following the road to priesthood, he attended St. John's University in Minnesota. As he continued to discern his vocation, he felt that the life of a parish priest/pastor would be too busy and hectic for him, and that perhaps he would be more suited to become a religious order priest. That is, a priest who lives and works with other priests in a communal setting, focused on a particular mission and way of life. Thus, he transferred to Crosier Seminary to pursue that path.

At a retreat (an extended period of prayer and discernment) during his first year of study, he came across a booklet which described the different contemplative religious orders/communities in the Church, and he became interested in the monastic life. Something that sparked his interest in monasticism, even more, was a conversation he had with another student who had recently spent time with the Trappist monks at New Melleray Abbey in Iowa. As time went on, Fr. Robert began to feel more and more drawn to the monastic life of silence, fasting, prayer, and penance. He recalled quite clearly, "That is what I wanted to do."

During his second year at Crosier Seminary, he and another student made a retreat at the monastery of New Melleray, and that experience finally confirmed his call to the monastic life. After finishing up classes that semester in 1949, he moved on to join the monks in Iowa. A decade or so later, in 1963, Fr. Robert accompanied the Abbot of New Melleray on a visit to Assumption Abbey, in Ava, Missouri. Father recalls how he casually mentioned to the Abbot, "I wouldn't mind it there at Assumption Abbey." He thought nothing of his comment until the Abbot later decided to send him there for what was supposed to be a one year stay, while the Abbey was undergoing some changes. A few years later, in 1968, he was still there in the Ozark Mountains of Ava.

At this point in our conversation, while Father was reflecting on his roots, he stopped and noted that, even during his first days at New Melleray, he felt a deep calling to even more solitude. For those who are not familiar with Catholic monasticism, a Trappist monk lives in "community" with other monks, but his life is at the same time one of tremendous solitude and silence. It is a life that would truly drive most people of our busy, noisy, modern culture to insanity quite quickly. When Father mentioned that he felt he was called to *even more* solitude and silence, I was quite fascinated and surprised, to say the least.

As the story goes, it was in May of 1968 that Fr. Robert was given permission by his superiors to live as a hermit. One of the other monks helped him build a very small, simple, shack-like hermitage way up on top of one of the surrounding Ozark hills deep in the woods. He would have no electricity, running water, or much of anything to provide physical comfort, by modern standards. When all was eventually in order, and after an accidental fire that almost burned his new home to the ground, Father, at last, moved in.

After just a few years of finally being able to live the solitary life that he longed for and truly felt called to, he was asked to come back down off the mountain. In May of 1971, it was requested of him to be the superior of the community back at the monastery, and so in the following year, he was elected Abbot. He was re-elected to this leadership position once more in the early '80s, but in 1986, he "finally had enough" and was able to go back to his beloved hermitage. Though he has lived in a couple of different hermitages over the years since then, he has continued full time in the eremitic life ever since.

Fr. Robert said to me that the reason he wanted to go into the hermitage and live in the wilderness in the first place was, "To really feel and experience true loneliness. In doing so, I would turn to God and develop a life of prayer, or I would start climbing the walls. However, when I got there, it felt like home, there was a great sense of peace and it's been that way ever since. That's how I knew that this was my vocation from God and I no longer had any doubts."

Fr. Robert's original hermitage, hidden deep within the Ozark Mountains of Missouri.

Q & A with a Hermit Monk

After listening to Fr. Robert's most interesting background story, I tried to focus in on more specific questions that I wanted to ask him about regarding his life of solitude in nature and his vocation. What follows is an account of our conversation.

Joe: "How would you describe the monastic life: its nature, purpose & mission?"

Fr. Robert: "The purpose of the monastic life is to be at the heart of the Church, to pray for the entire world, for missionaries everywhere, to offer penance (reparation for the sins of the world), but more than that, and most importantly, to give glory to God. Everything else that we do flows from our purpose of glorifying God."

Joe: "When you entered the monastic life, did you have any specific goals or expectations?"

Fr. Robert: "Well, when I entered, I expected the worst. (Laughs). Actually, I was looking forward to 'dying to self.' Even as a young kid, I was fed up with the 'world.' I don't know what it was. I came here to 'die a happy death.' I realized, first of all, that it was God's calling for me. That this is the way he wanted me to live. However, even at the beginning of my vocation, I realized that I was being called to the eremitic life, so what happens? I get out of the novitiate (an introductory training program) after six months, and I was put in as a sub-master for the new novices. At the time, New Melleray was very large, so I had to take care of all the exterior and material needs of the novices. This required a lot of talking back and forth (only with them of course) and so I realized that my dream of being a book on a shelf, never touched, never opened, and never looked at, was going to go down the drain (laughter).

When the superior announced that I was going to be the sub-master, I just dropped! It felt like the floor went out from under me. I was angry because I knew my life was going to be so involved. After the meeting with the superior when I was made sub-master, I went into the room where the novices were and saw a picture on the desk which said, 'In God We Trust,' and I was so mad that I took that picture, threw it in the waste can and walked out. (More laughs) I was really upset! So, about an hour later, I came back, took the picture out of the trashcan and everything was fine. I resolved that this was God's will for me at the time, and I became quite happy with it all."

Joe: "What have been the most fulfilling and the most challenging aspects of monastic life for you?"

Fr. Robert: "I can sum it up in one word, community. That aspect is the most fulfilling, and at the same time, the most challenging. (Laughs). It's true! It's a blessing and it's a curse. The challenging part of it is that it makes you more Christ-like. It takes the negative things out of you. It makes you realize where you have to grow, and then you become what you are supposed to be. Still, I've always been happy in the monastic life. The eremitic vocation has simply been an outgrowth of the monastic life. St. Benedict in his Rule (the classic handbook for western monasticism) states that after one has been in the monastic life for a number of years and then feels they have an eremitic vocation, they should be allowed to pursue it."

Joe: "What are some of the doubts, worries, or fears that you've experienced in your particular vocation and way of life?"

Fr. Robert: "One of my biggest fears is to have to go back to the community life and being drawn out of the hermitage, but that hasn't happened. We are a small community and they have always respected my vocation. I guess….hmmm…I don't really have any fears. Even if Assumption Abbey would have to close for some reason, well then, I guess we have to close. It's whatever God wants. If he wants us to close, then we'll do so. If he wants us to keep going, then we'll keep going. Whatever he wants is fine. Whenever any kind of fear or worry comes up, I just surrender it to the will of God. That's where my peace is."

The Eremitic Life

Another view of Fr. Robert's original hermitage.

At this point in our conversation, I wanted to focus more precisely on Father's vocation and life as a hermit living in the wilderness. Here is what followed…

Joe: "To shift gears a little bit now, I'd like to talk about your life more specifically as a hermit. For starters, how would you define the term 'hermit'?"

Fr. Robert: "I call myself an 'iconoclastic hermit.' The *iconoclastic heresy* of old was the mistaken idea that all religious images were 'idols,' and so there was the notion of destroying them, of getting rid of them all, no more pictures or statues of Jesus, Mary, or the saints, you know. And so, I kind of use that term to describe myself in that, I wanted to destroy all the 'images' of a hermit that anyone ever held…including myself. It's not good to try to live up to an image, because you can never do it, so I came to live life as I saw it, at each moment."

Joe: "Could you elaborate a little bit more about living in community life? What was the most motivating factor for you to separate yourself from the community and live in total solitude in the wilderness?"

Fr. Robert: "There was nothing about community life, with the brothers that drove me away. There was just always this need for more solitude. I wanted to have more silence, more prayer. Not that you can't do it in the monastery, or even outside in the 'world,' because we have to, everybody has to, but I felt that I had to have a quieter place for my particular needs."

Joe: "Could you describe for me a day in the life of a hermit? What does your average day entail?"

Fr. Robert: "On my average day, I get up at 1:00 AM. I find that the morning is the best time for praying. It's quiet, even nature is quiet at that time. So, I spend the first couple of hours in prayer, but that depends on how the Spirit is moving. Sometimes I'll spend four hours or so in prayer instead of two or three. That time is not always spent in 'prayer' (in the purest sense of the word) but I'm always there, and I have the Blessed Sacrament here, so I find that to be a tremendous help. (The Blessed Sacrament is the consecrated bread used during the celebration of Mass, which Catholics believe contains the true presence of Jesus Christ.)

Along with that, I have pretty much the same prayer schedule as they do down at the monastery. (A monk's day is structured around set times of prayer called the *Divine Office* or *Liturgy of the Hours*. The hours go by such names as *Vigils, Terce, Compline, Vespers*, etc.) So, after my four hours of prayer, I'll come down (he has a little loft area in his hermitage where he prays) and do a little exercise. Then I'll go into vigils, which will take me about thirty to forty-five minutes, then after that, I'll come back down again and eat breakfast, which is not much, some bread and an apple. I stopped drinking coffee long ago (laughs).

After breakfast, I'll go outside, pray the rosary and do a few things around here, and then I'll say Morning Prayer, followed by Mass. I use that desk over there for an altar too. About a half-hour after Mass, I'll say Terce, followed by some reading till about 10:30 AM, and then it will be time for my mid-day prayer and dinner at 11:00 AM. After dinner, I'll clean up my dishes, and if I haven't said a rosary by then, I'll go ahead and pray it, or do some more reading till about 2:00 PM. In the afternoon, I work. I'm a nut sorter, I've been sorting 'nuts' all my life (laughs) so I guess I'm pretty good at it by now. Really, I sort nuts, pecans, walnuts, etc., for the fruitcake bakery at the monastery, and I also do the laundry for the guest house on Saturdays. After my afternoon work, I'll pray Vespers, have supper, do some more reading, and by 6:30 PM, pray Compline and go to bed around 7:00 PM. So basically, I plan what time I'm going to get up, when to go to bed, what I'm going to eat, and the rest of the time is filled with prayer, work, and other things."

Joe: "We talked a little bit about what has brought you satisfaction and joy in the monastic life, but what more specifically as a hermit living in nature has brought you the greatest joy?"

Fr. Robert: "My prayer life. But I experience more and more what St. Teresa experienced: that dryness at times. It's all a part of faith, the Lord continues to come through even in those dry times. There is a little saying that I keep in mind in such times; 'Our *faith to face* vision of God is like a shining light that grows in brightness until we experience our *face to face* vision of God.' But in order to grow in brilliance, it has to be exercised. And that is why God withdraws himself at times, so you can exercise your faith. But every time you go through that dryness, the brilliance of God's presence becomes stronger and your experience of him becomes more profound too."

Joe: "Specifically as a hermit, what's been the most difficult/challenging thing about living in solitude out here in the wilderness?"

Fr. Robert: "I've never really found anything difficult about it. Like I mentioned, being called away from the hermitage years ago was very hard, but that's been it."

Joe: "We talked about the primary mission and purpose of the monastic life; praying and doing penance for the world, glorifying God, etc. What would you say is the primary mission and purpose of an eremitic vocation, living as a hermit? Is there more of a focus on any of those areas?"

Fr. Robert: "It's pretty much the same, but much more intense."

Joe: "Here is a very common question that priests and individuals in religious vocations get asked often, and I'm sure people are wondering even more so about your particular way of life. 'Do you get lonely?' What would you say is the difference between loneliness and solitude?"

Fr. Robert: "Loneliness, I've never really experienced. I constantly keep my communication going with the Lord, and so in other words, I'm not alone, I have the Lord with me, and that's what solitude is. Before I entered New Melleray Abbey, my sister asked me why I would ever want to join the Trappists since I like to talk so much. (Laughs) It's just one of those things, I guess."

Joe: "You mentioned that you work down at the monastery at certain times. In the midst of that, do you interact much with the community down there? Do you see family or deal much with the public or the outside world?"

Fr. Robert: "I go to the Benedictine monastery in Subiaco, Arkansas, about four times a year now to be available to the monks if they want to talk. It helps to have someone from outside their community to talk about things at times. With family, I've gone home several times over the years and they can come and visit, but there has to be some reason for me to go. I don't just leave for a 'vacation' of some kind."

Joe: "There are many religious as well as secular individuals who over the years have pursued a solitary life in order to discover things like the 'core of who they are,' what truly makes them happy, what the ultimate purpose of their existence is, and things of that sort. How would you respond, or describe those ideals for yourself?"

Fr. Robert: "Well, first of all, I didn't come here for myself. I came to find, and to be with Christ. That has been my focus. But in that process, you find out who you are, you see who and what you truly are. So, my main focus is on Christ, but through him it comes back to me, to become more Christ-like. Seeking Christ is the joy of my life. Without that, I might as well not be here."

Joe: "The major criticism of those who pursue a religious vocation, and especially those individuals (either religious or secular) who live a solitary life hidden away in the wilderness, is that it is a form of escapism, that it is a selfish lifestyle, that they are running away from something. What would your response to that be?"

Fr. Robert: "That's true. For some, it can be a form of escapism. But as an Abbot once told me, 'You'll have to ask the Holy Spirit about it. He's the one who called me to this life.' (Laughs). That's why you have to really discern your vocation. Because there is so much of that going on, escapism, especially nowadays, we see it here. But the more I hear about what's going on outside in the world, about the 'communication explosion,' it's going to be harder for younger people to come in (to a monastic/solitary life) and really settle down. Young people are in contact with their friends 24 hours a day with all the phones and pictures and all those things. For a person to enter into this kind of life today, it would have to be a person who is fed up with all the gadgetry, and also a person who is sure of why he is pursuing this life. If it's just because he's fed up, it will never work. But if he's fed up because it is keeping him from a deeper way of life, then he can start looking at it."

Joe: "What is the most important insight or lesson you've learned in your life thus far as a monk, a priest, and a hermit living in nature?"

Fr. Robert: "Perseverance. Not just perseverance, but perseverance with a steadfast heart, faithful spirit, and heartfelt devotion. You can persevere at something by just dragging your feet with your chin on the ground, (laughs) but it really needs to be the other way. Perseverance is the hardest thing to do, with any way of life, especially married life."

Joe: "There is the perception that religious, monks, hermits, etc., encounter or experience the divine, as well as evil, in more direct ways than those 'in the world.' Could you describe how you experience and encounter God, as well as evil, in your life?"

Fr. Robert: "An important distinction, first of all, is that in my prayer life, I'm not here to necessarily *experience* God, but to *worship* God and to give myself to him. If he wants to manifest himself to me in a particular way, that's fine. If not, that's fine too. That's a tough lesson to learn. As far as evil, you really do experience the evil in yourself when you are seeking God. You see all the negative things in you, and that can be disturbing (laughs) to say the least! It's in us, the anger, jealousy, lust, and all the rest of it. They call it the seven capital sins in the Church, but the early monastic fathers called it the 'eight logi,' or, eight thoughts, which include gluttony, lust, things (materialism), anger, dejection, sloth, vanity, and pride. We all face that battle.

Spiritual combat, that's what the monastic life is all about, fighting the evil that is within us. There was a song that I always kept in mind before going into the monastery, and I still reflect on it now: 'Accentuate the positive, eliminate the negative, and don't mess around with Mr. In-between.' (Laughs) You get rid of the negative by emphasizing the positive, by working on love. By doing that, the evil in you gradually leaves you. It's like oil and water. The oil stays on top, but if you pour enough water in, the oil eventually is forced out by the overflow of water. So again, accentuating love is what gets rid of the evil."

Joe: "That's a neat analogy, I like that! Here is a question someone had in mind for me to ask you, how has your life of solitude helped you to effectively demonstrate the love of God?"

Fr. Robert: "By being present to God, by being faithful and recollected in my vocation. And of course by sharing his love with others when I'm at the monastery, with visitors, etc. That's one of the good things about having to go back to the monastery and having to communicate with others at times. It's another opportunity to share that love."

Joe: "Here's a very simple question many are curious about. Do you keep in touch with the current state of the world, with political, social, and cultural issues?"

Fr. Robert: "I really don't. I can recall how back home when my dad would be listening to the news, afterward he'd get very upset! (Laughs)."

Joe: "Yeah, my dad does the same thing! (Laughs)."

Fr. Robert: "If there is anything that has to be known, I'll hear about it. But I don't have a TV, or a radio, or anything like that. The more thoughts you get in your mind, the harder they are to get out, especially at times of prayer. With all the advertising that goes on now, you can't look at anything without being bombarded with useless information. I don't have a need for any of that. I don't feel the need for a computer or a phone, or any of that. I have a phone (laughs) but I rarely use it. I don't need a 1-800 number to call God (laughs). If I were a writer, I could see where a computer would come in handy, but since I'm not, I just don't have a need for it."

Joe: "To switch gears a little, by means of our baptism in the Church, we as Christians believe that we are called to share in the life and ministry of Jesus as 'priest, prophet, and king.' How do you fulfill those as a hermit living in nature?"

Fr. Robert: "Well, I do offer Mass every day."(Laughs).

Joe: "Yes, well, the 'priest' part is obvious, but what about the other two areas of prophet and king?"

Fr. Robert: "I suppose that my way of life is how I live out the call to be a 'prophet,' it's countercultural. (Thinks in silence for a moment). I guess I really don't consciously concentrate on how I fulfill those roles. I just focus on what I'm supposed to be doing here, my life of prayer and being with the Lord. I don't think in terms of all those categories, to put it that way."

Joe: "In Luke 8:11-15, we read about the parable of the seed and the sower. What aspect of your life chokes out the Word of God? What doesn't allow God's voice to take root?"

Fr. Robert: "All those distracting thoughts that we talked about. That's the big one. You can't help it. For me, it's thoughts of the past or the future. You can't help but think about such things, of course, but I do. It's mainly thoughts of things in my past life. Sometimes, when I go down to the monastery, I'll have these thoughts of past experiences or I'll hear something from someone, and those kinds of things can come in and choke the word out."

Joe: "There is a commonly held notion that the joy and happiness in our lives are only real, or of value, when it is shared with others, and that human relationships are the most essential component of our lives. As one who lives in the solitude of nature, what are your thoughts on that?"

Fr. Robert: "Do you believe in Jesus Christ?"

Joe: "Yes."

Fr. Robert: "True man and true God?"

Joe: "Yes."

Fr. Robert: "There is my human interaction." (Laughs with an affirmative tone). Those are certainly legitimate concerns, but if you have been called to a life of solitude in order to develop a closer relationship with God, that relationship reaches a fullness in the living out of that call."

Joe: "As we know, the ultimate expression of the love of Christ is a self-sacrificing love, sharing it with others and giving it away. What is your primary avenue of sharing the self-sacrificing love of Christ out here in the solitude of the wilderness?"

Fr. Robert: "That is a challenge that comes to mind every once in a while, the social aspect of sharing God's love with others, helping the poor, etc. And that is what the community is about. To love and serve each other and to give charity, as a community, to those in need. We give at least 10 percent of what we earn (from the bakery) to charity. But as far as the hands-on aspect, that is one of the big temptations at times that draws people out of the monastery, especially younger people. That's why one has to be convinced that this is their vocation, that God has called them to this. If he wants you to be out in the world doing some hands-on work, he will make it known to you. Our prayer, fasting, and penance are our 'work,' and the expression of our love for the world."

The Spirituality of a Hermit

For this final phase of our visit, I asked Fr. Robert some questions on the subject of prayer and spirituality. Here is what he had to say on the matter....

Joe: "As we know, there are lots of theologians who write on the topics of prayer and spirituality, and there are thousands of books on the subject, but how would you personally define spirituality?"

Fr. Robert: "(Laughs) How would I define spirituality? (Laughs some more) By simply finding time to live for the Lord. (Pauses to reflect for a few moments) Our Lord, in speaking to the Samaritan woman, said that there will come a time when you 'worship in spirit and in truth.' I was thinking about that the other day, and it came to me while celebrating Mass. When I raised the chalice up, that this is what I do, live in Jesus, with Jesus, through Jesus, in the unity of the Holy Spirit. That's the essence of my spiritual life. Prayer then, is simply being in the life of God"

Joe: "What styles, forms, or expressions of prayer do you most utilize and gravitate to in your vocation as a monk and as a hermit?"

Fr. Robert: "The rosary is my constant source of 'vocal prayer' along with the Mass and the office of course. But most of my prayer is just quiet prayer, being silent with God."

Joe: "Along with that then, could you talk about the importance of silence?"

Fr. Robert: "We need silence so we can hear what is going on in ourselves…what is really going on. That's why I think so many people always have to have music or something going in the background to constantly distract them, so they can't hear themselves. To truly come to know yourself, and to do so well, takes silence. There has to be silence to be able to hear what the Lord is saying."

Joe: "As a hermit, what are your greatest joys and struggles with prayer?"

Fr. Robert: "The greatest struggle is the dryness that comes at times. There are often long periods of dryness, but of course, the joys come too, like dew on the dry grass. But as I mentioned earlier, you have to persevere in that. You have to keep going forward steadily with it, no matter how you feel. That's an important thing. We can't live our lives just on feelings. They are important, but we can't base our lives (especially spiritual lives) on them. Faith is what is important, and living by faith can be a pretty hard thing to do at times."

Joe: "To bring things to a close, what would your words of wisdom be for the person living 'in the world' with all its fast-paced craziness that we experience in our present day?"

Fr. Robert: "In scripture, Jesus asks the rhetorical question, 'Do you think that when I come I will find faith?' Faith is the most important thing in our life. No matter how busy we are, we have to maintain our faith in God and not let it go. 'Do you think I will find faith?' There are so many things outside that are drawing us away from faith. We have to come back to it, and that is where spending time in solitude comes in, to get back to our roots. If we lose our faith, we've lost everything. So, no matter how busy you are in your life, you have to find some time to get some solitude and silence and get back to your roots with the Lord."

Fr. Robert: "Have you ever heard of Catherine de Hueck Doherty? Here is something she wrote." (At this point Father hands me a dusty, old, tattered and stain covered cardboard picture frame with these words in the center:)

"Remember that you are going to the desert for the following reasons:

-To fast.
-To live in silence.
-To pray.
-So that you might die to yourself quicker, so that Christ might grow in you faster.
-So that you might give him to the world faster too, this world that is so hungry for him.
-To atone for your sins and those of others.
-To pray for all humanity.
-To pray for peace.
-To pray for the mission and unity amongst Christians in the Church.
-To become saints faster, i.e., lovers of Christ in truth and in deed.
-To imitate Christ.

-To save your soul and those of others.
-To learn total surrender to Christ quicker.

We have made him wait long enough!"

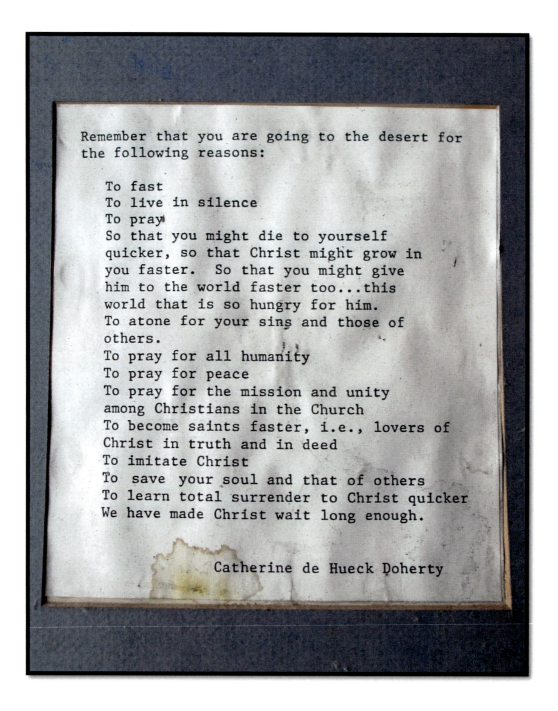

Fr. Robert: "That would be a summation of what I have come to do. In a nutshell, that's what I'm all about."

Joe: "Excellent! Any concluding thoughts you'd like to share?"

Fr. Robert: "To make God number one in your life. He's got to be number one, not number two. Even in married life, he has to be number one. He is what holds you together. If he isn't there, everything will fall apart. There is no substitute!"

Back to the World

With Fr. Robert's final words of wisdom resonating in my heart, our time together had come to an end and I found myself beginning my journey home, back to the "world" of civilization. As I drove over the hills and through the woods of the Missouri Ozark Mountains, I was filled with a spirit of peace and refreshment. I was extremely grateful for being able to spend time in the stunning beauty of the area, but much more so, to experience the beauty of the wisdom I had encountered in this wise, old monk of the wilderness.

As I have shared throughout this book, there is an incarnate wisdom to be found in the wild, but in the case of my time with Fr. Robert, that wisdom was *truly incarnate*: manifested and embodied in the gentle soul of this monk who lived alone in nature.

My time with this holy man was a great reminder about the many life lessons learned in the wilderness. Fr. Robert is a living witness and a prophetic voice who teaches us that nature, *in and of itself*, is not what we seek as human beings, but rather, what happens in the solitude of nature is what we long for and crave. We seek connectedness with creation, but much more so, whether consciously or unconsciously, we seek connectedness with our Creator. It's interesting to note that the word "religion" actually means, literally, to "reconnect," as that is the point of it all. It's this reconnection with God, God's creation, one another, and ourselves, that brings about a great awakening and a renewal of our nature as human beings.

All of the good that we seek in creation is ultimately found in God, who is its source. While the presence of God can certainly be found and experienced in the solitude of nature, where worldly distractions are greatly minimized, our Creator is found most perfectly in the love which is present in the human heart. This love is the masterpiece of God's creation. The human heart was not created to be indifferent, but rather, it is a dwelling meant to be filled with goodness, truth, freedom, wisdom, compassion, peace, joy, and every positive virtue, as these are the things which fill our beings, and our world, with life and love. This is the paradise that we seek and long for. It is found in exploring the vast wilderness of the human soul, whose beauty knows no bounds. Upon finding it, experiencing it, and sharing it, we come to echo the words of St. Paul, "Eye has not seen and ear has not heard what God has planned for those who love him." This is the love, which patiently waits to be awakened within us all.

Share the Journey!

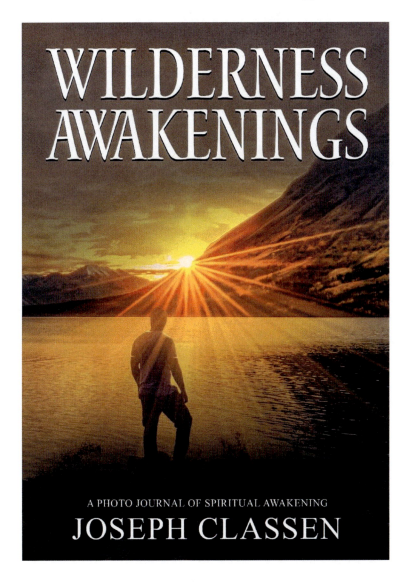

Order additional copies of Wilderness Awakenings at Amazon.com or Wild Revelation Outdoors

Don't Miss Out on All the Adventure!

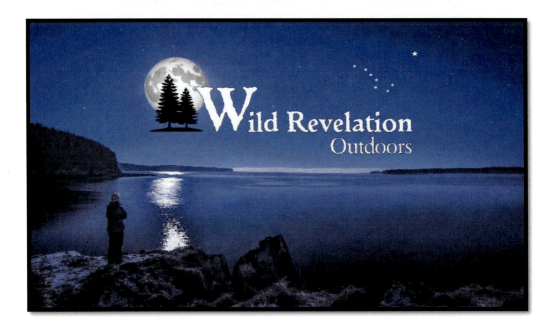

Wild Revelation Outdoors produces a wide variety of entertaining, educational, and inspirational multimedia, as well as operates an Alaskan guide and adventure/travel consultation service. Additionally, we feature an online Amazon affiliate store where one can shop *exclusively* for the most dependable, highest quality outdoor products on the market from the most reliable, proven brands in the world.

Visit us today at www.wildrevelation.com

Made in the USA
Middletown, DE
15 January 2020